THE NEW CURATE

First published in 1997 by
Mercier Press
PO Box 5, 5 French Church Street Cork
16 Hume Street Dublin 2
Trade enquiries to CMD Distribution
55A Spruce Avenue
Stillorgan Industrial Park
Blackrock County Dublin

© Christy Kenneally 1997

ISBN 1 85635 199 8

10 9 8 7 6 5 4 3 2

A CIP record for this title is available
from the British Library

Cover design by Penhouse Design
Set by Richard Parfrey
Printed in Ireland by ColourBooks
Baldoyle Industrial Estate, Dublin 13

Published in the US and Canada by
the Irish American Book Company
6309 Monarch Park Place, Niwot,
Colorado, 80503
Tel: (303) 530-1352, (800) 452-7115
Fax: (303) 530-4488, (800) 401-9705.

THE NEW CURATE

CHRISTY KENNEALLY

MERCIER PRESS

About the Author

Christy Kenneally was born in 1948 in Cork's Northside. He was ordained to the priesthood for the diocese of Cork and Ross in 1973 and appointed chaplain to St Patrick's Hospital after a short time as a curate in his home parish. In 1979 he left the priesthood and is now married with two children and living in County Wicklow.

He has published two books of poetry under the Gilbert Dalton imprint: *The Joseph Coat and Other Patches* and *Out Foreign and Back.* Under the imprint of Paulist Press, USA, he has published two books of poetry for children: *Strings and Things* (winner of the CPA award for best children's book) and *Miracles and Me.* A book of reflections, entitled *Passio,* was published by Veritas in 1995.

With Mercier Press he published a bestselling book of memoirs, *Maura's Boy,* in 1996.

Christy Kenneally is the director of a communications training company, devising and implementing communications training workshops at home and abroad. He is internationally acknowledged as an expert in the area of communicating with people in crisis. In this respect he is the author of two audio tapes: *Communicating with the Sick and Dying* and *Sorry for Your Trouble, Helping the Bereaved.*

To the men and women of
St Patrick's Hospital, Cork (1973–76)
who led me to the heart of love,
and to my wife and children who live there

CONTENTS

CONTENTS

1

THE PREMATURE PRIEST

When I stand naked before Him,
a carrion name
and cancerous with failure,
He will look gently upon me
and wryly smile a welcome.
For clowns are His special children
who laugh that they may not weep
and ease men's yoke a little
as they pass.

I was a premature priest.

In the year 1973, Cornelius, by the grace of God and favour of the Apostolic See, Bishop of Cork and Ross, sat down to rotate his clergy. He found his perfect plan was foiled for the want of a single curate. Pragmatic as ever, he decided to make one. Me!

It never occurred to him that the Maynooth authorities might have something to say about their deacon being ordained a few months shy of the seven regulatory years. We had our own pope in Cork. When the small man with the bushy eyebrows railed against the government of the day at the haemorrhage of people from the land, we said, 'Sure he's the boy for them!' It didn't faze us that he made his thundering denouncements at Confirmation ceremonies to a congregation wilting in white dresses or strangling in new suits. Their biggest theological and social questions were: 'When do we get the clatter?' or 'How much money will we make?' Cornelius was following in a long line of episcopal 'disturbers' from Delaney through Coughlan. The former was reported to initiate clerical changes by saying, 'Give me me pen till I scatter them.' The latter, hearing on his deathbed that the Protestant bishop had predeceased him, whispered with some satisfaction, 'Now he knows who's Bishop of Cork.'

Naturally, I was the last to know. After all, a deacon was about one step above an altar boy in the hierarchy of the Church. He could bless bread and baptise babies but anyone who had reached 'the use of reason' could do that. In matters of notification, I fell into the limbo category between those he might favour with a phone call and those who would receive only the handwritten pale-blue envelope that could raise the blood pressure of many a comfortable curate.

The call came to Maynooth from the Vocations Director of the diocese. In a formal voice he said his Lordship would ordain me on the fourteenth of April and because the official ordinations would happen in June, I would be 'done' in a convent chapel. This should have been the greatest anticlimax of my life. After all, in theory I had been preparing for ordination for the best part of seven years. But I was still shell-shocked. In reality, Maynooth had become a world and life of itself and now, standing in a cubicle under the stairs, I realised it was over. When the shock wore off I made a call to a priest of the diocese who had been my friend and mentor from secondary school. Then I called the Vocations Director.

'Father, please tell his Lordship that I will be happy to be ordained on the fourteenth of April. However, I consider my ordination as official as any other and I would like to be ordained in my home parish, the cathedral.'

Within the hour, he was back on the line to say the bishop had said yes. I was always a nice rather than an assertive boy but I had been reared by an independent man. Years before, his Lordship sent a messenger to my father to say he had organised a scholarship so that a society would pay our portion of the college fees and the bishop would pay his. The messenger made two mistakes. He refused a cup of tea at the oilcloth-covered table and he misjudged the calibre of the man he was talking to.

'Tell the bishop I'm grateful for his offer but the society can pay his share of the fees and I'll pay mine.'

Then he courteously showed him to the door. He belonged to a generation that 'had their pride'. If it couldn't be paid for then it wouldn't be got. And if we needed help we would go to 'our own'. When I asked him about it, all he would say was, 'I wouldn't have a child of mine beholden to anyone. You'll always have your independence.' As a widower and a factory worker with three other children, he could have done with the help, but his home was his castle and his children his treasure. Cork and Ross could pay for their priest; he would pay for his son.

Before any great event, people take refuge in rituals. Soldiers check their equipment and write inadequate love letters they pray may never be delivered. Hurlers band a hurley, fold a knee bandage or pack and repack a gear bag, keeping the mind at bay with mechanical tasks. What do deacons do? I remember needlessly polishing my brand new shoes and checking the soles for price tags. As a former altar boy, I could recall more than one bridegroom who had snared our attention with a tag for seventeen and six when he knelt to take his vows. 'She's getting a right bargain there,' some wag would whisper. The black socks, a present from Purcell's, were rolled and snuggled into the shoes; the plastic collar, scrubbed with Parazone, coiled whiter than white on the bedside locker; the soutane, stippled down the front with bright buttons, hung deflated on the door, waiting for the man to fill it in the morning. This would be my last night sleeping in Pop's house, two doors up from my own. This room had become mine during the holidays from Maynooth so that I wouldn't wake to Michael rolling in from the Arcadia ballroom late at night or Dave rolling out to the Hanover shoe factory early in the morning.

Auntie Eily and her husband Pat Daly made a succession of night suppers – 'Sure we'll have one more cuppa before the stairs' – as if we were holding fast to something we sensed would change and be lost forever. Finally we checked and double-checked that all my gear was ready for the day. The old house groaned and leant against its neighbours for comfort as up and down the lane our ritual was mirrored in the small houses where 'good clothes' were laid out and curlers were rolled in before the doors were banged and locked. As I lay in Pop's bed, Shandon tolled the end of day. I tried to pray for the souls of the dead: for Maura my mother and Pop and Nan and Auntie Nelly Dorgan, but the memories welled from the walls and drowned my prayers.

I am back again with Michael by the fire as the old women wail for my dead mother; raised from sleep at the bottom of the stairs at Eily's twenty-first, sick from sweets and bursting with Tanora, to be ferried off to bed in Uncle Paddy's arms. I am hit-and-missing my way two-fingered through 'The Minstrel Boy' on the piano or sitting companionably, an empty briar stuck in my mouth, as Pop blows smoke rings like a Red Indian message from behind the *Echo*. Much later, turning the awkward corner of fourteen, I am soaking up the books for the Inter Cert at the table by the window, safe from the seduction of boys with hurleys calling at number six to lure me out to play. And always, I am swinging like the needle of a compass to the pole star sitting in the corner, secure in the knowledge that though my firmament had suffered more than its share of black holes, he would continue to shine, steady and true.

The aurora of memory shifts in the darkness and I am ten. We climb into pyjamas in the night light. Beyond the window, the grass of the quarry is brittle with frost; every humble puddle sports a silver moon. 'We'll say our prayers in bed,' he says, in deference to the lino's sting. I absolve myself with the thought that the holy souls have waited millions of years for the pardon of our prayers and another hundred days won't make a difference.

'Pop.'

'What, boy?'

'I'm frightened, Pop.'

'Of what, alanna?'

'The woman in the picture is watching me.'

'Arrah, sure that's only St Anne, Our Lady's mother. She won't do you a bit of harm.'

'But her eyes are looking at me.'

'Suffering God, 'tis only the way the picture is made. Close your eyes now and I'll give out the Rosary.'

I curl into the curve of his back, my feet questing for the warm pocket behind his knees. 'The first Sorrowful Mystery, the Agony in the Garden. Ah, Saint Anthony, your feet are frozen. Our Father . . . ' Like two oarsmen, we rhythmically Hail and Holy Mary into the dark until the old man takes the strain for both of us and I am rocked to silence by the smooth sweep of supplication. One night, right at the threshold of sleep, I asked, 'Pop, sure you won't die?'

'No, boy,' he replied strongly. 'I won't die.'

And I believed him. I continued to clutch that promise through the fall from the barracks roof that shattered his leg into eight pieces, and through the heart attacks that pulled him down so that my head bobbed above his and mine was the arm he leant on. I believed it up to the day the dean called me from the noise of the Maynooth refectory to say, 'A grandfather of yours has died.'

And now, lying in the same bed the night before my ordination, I curl up and stretch my feet to where he would have been. Pop, I'm frightened, is my last thought.

On the day, there was one final ritual to be performed. Auntie Eily washed my hair in the sink. Her baby was overdue so she wouldn't be in the congregation. 'With all the excitement, we might get more than we bargained for. I'll sit here and start my prayers when I hear the bell. D'ye know, you have loads of grey hairs?' she said, starting a banter for both our sakes.

'Better grey than green.'

'True enough, boy! 'Tis a bad tree won't blossom.'

She worked the shampoo into my scalp with a rare tenderness and I knew that this was the last simple intimate service a woman of my tribe could do for me. I was glad of the excuse of suds in my eyes when I raised my head to the towel.

'Shave carefully now, boy, and don't disgrace us with pieces of the *Examiner* stuck to your face.'

Nearly a quarter of a century has passed since that day. My memories are like sparks from the fire that flare unexpectedly, but they are always the same. I remember Paddy the sacristan, checking and rechecking the oils and keeping a wary eye on the spotless finger-towel reserved for the bishop, in case some grubby altar boy would leave his imprimatur on it. My white alb and cincture looked suitably humble among the cloth of gold the main con-celebrants would wear. Occasionally Paddy would kneel up beside me at the window bench, keeping me company as we watched people file towards the church doors. Gradually the sacristy began to fill. The canons of the diocese came with their fur-trimmed garb and formed a purple pool at one end. Assisting curates in plain black soutanes and spotless surplices handed out copies of the rituals and chivied the altar boys to line up with the cross and candles. There was a palpable air of expectation in the room; then the door swung open and the bishop walked in. Though a small man, he had an aura that extended before him and quenched the murmur of talk. As if he sensed the effect his entrance made, he smiled and engaged one of the canons in conversation. The talk resumed, but more muted than before.

'How're you feeling?' he asked as we approached the bench.

'I'm fine, my lord,' I lied.

'Good boy!'

As the bishop dressed, Paddy unsheathed the two ends of the crozier and screwed them together, handing it to him only after he had donned the mitre. Paddy then stood behind me as I threw the folds of the alb over my head, catching the hem and pulling it down. Then he held the cincture taut behind me so that I could swing it into a loop at my waist. For a moment he pressed his palm between my shoulder blades as if saying goodbye to the boy he had known. At last, on the first stroke of the clock, we moved in solemn procession to the church. The choir surged into a Latin motet from the balcony and there was something unbelievably comforting in hearing the Latin sung in unmistakable Cork accents.

In the solemn sway of the procession, against a background of blurred faces, my mind went again to Pop. He rarely spoke of the war against the Tans. When he was cajoled into a story, it was usually about something trivial.

'We were told never to use a comrade's name, in case the Tans would hear it and trace him. Well, we were involved in a bit of a ... eh ... tussle like and they were after us. Now there was a low-sized fella from the Terrace and his nickname was Toy. And as we were harin' down Gerald Griffin Street he started to go astray. Paddy Dullea shouted after him, "Toy, Toy!" When he caught up with us he was foamin' at Paddy for using his name and he shouted at the top of his voice, "Paddy Dullea, Paddy Dullea!"'

I was disappointed and amazed. Disappointed because he hadn't told us the real stuff like did he shoot a Tan and did he take half an hour to fall down and die like the fellas in the pictures. I was amazed that all he could remember from these heart-stopping moments were the funny bits. And yet, maybe that's how people cope in moments of high tension; they seize on something inconsequential to block out their fears.

I remember lying flat on the floor of the altar as a litany of saints and martyrs with unlikely names was intoned over me, and thinking, did I double-check the soles of my shoes for labels. I remember, when the monsignor declared that 'upon enquiry among the people of God' I was deemed worthy of ordination, wondering who did they ask. Hardly the owners of the windows I had smashed with a football, or the woman who declared affectionately that I was 'a saucy caffler' and should 'be sent to Greenmount industrial school'. And certainly not Bina, our neighbour, who wasn't shy about saying that my brother Michael should have been the priest. These memories were what people would call distractions at their prayers, and yet on that day I felt that they were at the heart of my prayers, drawing me into the presence of a God who had revealed Himself to me through the lives of those who now filled the seats behind me.

I remember glimpses of faces on the altar. The lived-in face of the priest from Grawn who said a gruff and saintly Mass for my mother a couple of times a year, the man who had baptised me and then become my professor in Maynooth. One day in physiology class he shot a question at a sleeping student: 'What's the capacity of the bladder?'

Jerked by an elbow from his slumber, the student caught the prompt from behind. 'Twenty gallons, Doctor.'

'You should be in the fire brigade,' came the dry reply.

I remember the ecclesiastic who always managed to have a sour face in repose so that my grandfather had dubbed him Suck-a-Lemon. And time and time again, my eye was drawn to the round, reddened face of my mentor and friend, Father Harte, who was known to the boys of the Northside as 'Doc'. This was the man who had lent me Greene, Maugham, Waugh and Wodehouse, and who sent pages of stamps to Maynooth so that I could write to him. These are the threads I have left from the tapestry of light and music, wax and incense, question and response that was my ordination. And then, it was over.

In the sacristy there was a group photograph with the bishop. My father, grandmother and aunts representing both sides of the river gathered together. Instinctively I stood at my father's shoulder. 'No,' the bishop said firmly, 'the new priest must stand beside his bishop.' I glanced at my father's face as he struggled with his composure.

I sense now that my grandmother, who was a witness to this scene, felt deeply for the pain of her own child at that moment. For just then the bishop turned to her and asked, 'Are you proud to have a grandson a priest?'

In a rare show of public affection, she took my father's hand before replying, 'Indeed and I'm not, your Lordship, but I am proud to have reared a son who reared a priest.'

He laughed at that. What else could he do? He'd met his match in Katie Barrett.

2

THE HONEYMOON

The honeymoon started with goodbyes. I remember a sinking feeling as the friends from Maynooth piled into cars for the long journey back. For seven years I had lived on the draughty plains of Kildare, often driven by home-sickness to a top window for a glimpse of the Dublin mountains across that featureless, flat landscape, to remind me of the hills of home. But I had made my own of it in time, forging friendships and developing interests, finding a security in a life regulated by bells. And now, like many a traveller who has come at last to his desti-nation, I valued the journey more than the arrival. Cork was no longer a place for the holidays, where neighbours hailed me with that peculiar Cork greeting, 'You're home. When are you going back?' For a man who had left home for Farna, the minor seminary, at fifteen, this was not home and there would be no going back.

Officially, I was to be a curate in the cathedral until the bishop could juggle a niche for me somewhere in the diocese. A prophet in my own country, I was decorative rather than functional, too familiar to be taken seriously.

Reminders of my limbo status were all around me: in the old woman who stroked my face in Shandon Street and said, 'Sure I knew your poor mother Maura', or Paddy the sacristan in the flurry before Mass calling me 'Christy' and then correcting himself with my proper title. It was a time for grieving, for letting go of what I had known and learning from the new life what it was to be a priest.

Most curates and parish priests in the diocese lived alone, but the cathedral had a presbytery. It was a large draughty building with creaking wooden floors. The priests' rooms were at the top of the house and their individual kitchens and housekeepers were in the basement. I knew the geography of the place reasonably well. The front parlour was where we learned 'de Latin' from Father Cashman as altar boys, and where Towser, my pal, wondered why the Lamb of God should be called 'Agnes Daly'. Regular pilgrimages with Mass cards for signing or sprints at night for a priest for a dying neighbour had opened up the inner sanctum of this rabbit warren. It held no strangeness for me. It was my brother curates who were a bit distant towards the 'new fella'. The tidal wave of Vatican II was still surging through the church and, while some wanted to surf the freedom of the movement for change, others trod water or swam frantically against the current towards the firm ground of what had always been. That tension was evident among the clergy but it took a local woman to put words on the confusion and pain: 'Father, I preferred the Mass when I didn't understand a word of it.'

The church was caught in a whirlpool between the passing of what was familiar and cherished and the assimilation of what was new. Small wonder then that my brother priests should be a little wary of the latest product of a seminary that had changed so radically since their own day. I needed expert guidance; so I went to see Jim Keating.

Jim was an old neighbour who had been reared around the corner from our lane. He was brought up in a house that swelled to bursting with operatic arias from a scratchy gramophone. He had been 'head and tail' of the boys' club and the underage GAA competitions, and respected by all for his good humour and sense of fairness. He had also been a master carpenter until arthritis had twisted his fingers into the kind of knots that defied his saw. Over the years the passage of his illness took him through sticks to crutches and finally to the bed. Occasionally he made a foray in a wheelchair but it was a painful pilgrimage endured only for special occasions such as my ordination. Like a china teapot in the glass-case at home, his visitors handled him with exquisite care; even the slightest pressure on his fingers could flood his eyes. Jim's door was permanently 'on the push', his wife Bridget warm and welcoming, the teapot never cold. I found him napkined with a spread *Examiner*, enthroned on a mound of spotless pillows.

'God bless all here!'

'Come in outta that, ye dirty dog. Not comparin' you to the blessed animal.'

'Dear God,' Bridget said in mock horror, 'if anyone heard the two of ye!'

'How are ye, Jim?'

He held up a caricature of a hand. 'D'ye see that small

finger? That took a turn for the worse this mornin'.'

This was a familiar ritual of banter he used to put his visitors at their ease. Over the teacups I poured out my tensions and my shock at taking the men's confraternity the night before. In my youth the cathedral was always packed with men for the Rosary and sermon every Monday night, and I could recall the hairs standing on my head when they rose in full voice to sing 'We Stand for God'. The night before, I had looked down on a sea of empty spaces where islands of old men floated in the shadows.

'Did you ask them to move up the front?' he asked.

'Ah God no, Jim, sure they have their own places for years.'

'Good boy,' he said approvingly, bending his head to the cup he couldn't raise. 'Dere's good men above in that presbytery,' he said after a while. It was a Northside question couched as a statement.

'They're a bit wary of me, Jim. I don't know what to do.'

'Well now, I remember lads like that in the club – fellas who'd be watching you, trying to get your measure like. Sure as soon as we'd get an oul match going, they'd all pull together and be grand.'

The Holy Spirit had spoken and I was filled with inspiration.

'Jim?'

'What, boy?'

'Can I have a loan of the bowl?'

The twenty-eight ounce iron ball was a joke-present I had given him years before. He kept it in a drawer beside the gramophone, and sometimes, when he had visitors who didn't know his form and were inclined to lament his condition, he'd say, 'I threw a score of bowls against Mick Barry last Saturday.' This always put a brake on the comforters.

'Did ya, Jimmy boy?' they'd ask to humour him.

'I did faith, and I had one of the Shea boys from the Mon field to show me road.' They were speechless at this.

'He was a bowl of odds up on me when we reached the Viaduct. "Doubles or quits on the loft," says I. "You're on," says he. I left her loose and she sailed over like a swallow. Barry's bowl took a bit outta the bridge. "You're a better man than me, Jim Keating," says he. Bridget, show them the bowl there in the drawer.'

Bridget, a willing accomplice, reverently opened the drawer and there was the iron ball in a nest of clean hankies. The visitors would make their excuses fairly handy after that, leaving him laughing in the bed, the tears streaming down his face from the effort.

''Tis dere in the drawer, boy.'

'I think 'tis punctured.'

'Bridget, would you have a bit of steel wool? We'll have to patch the bowl.'

'You're worse than him,' she laughed, drenching me with holy water at the door. My heart soared as my pocket sagged. I had a twenty-eight ounce key to clerical integration.

'Bowling?'

'Yes.'

'God 'tis years since I threw a score.'

Kevin's tone was doubtful but his eyes were dancing. Donovan, big, broad and hearty, was game for anything.

'Who else could we get?'

Misery loves company. The following Wednesday we had two teams on the back Blarney road, dressed in the assortment of mismatched casual clothes that only celibates can manage. Kevin was rusty but he was a natural and soon swung into his rhythm. I watched him dance a little skip sideways before he wound into a short run. Then, hopping into the air, he loosed the bowl to spark sweet and true along the camber of the road, driving us up the ditch with wild cries.

'Doubt'ya boy, all the way.'

Coordination was not a word in Donovan's vocabulary. He had the mind and the muscle, but under separate contracts, and his run-up warned us of impending disaster. When he released the bowl we were already competing for available cover. It shot straight up in the air and landed in a field of cabbage.

'The bloody shooting season is over,' Murph grumbled from a tangle of briars.

We were wading shin-deep in green stalks when a woman's voice asked, 'And what do ye cafflers think ye're doing?'

She was standing at the back door of her bungalow like John Wayne, ready to draw.

'We're looking for the bowl, ma'am,' Kevin said lamely.

'Get yer arses and yer bowl outta my cabbage,' she roared. Then a shock of recognition shook through her as if a particularly heavy someone had walked over her grave.

'Oh, God bless us, Father, I'm very sorry. Will ye come in for the cup of tea?'

'Ah no thanks, ma'am; sure we've found it now, so we'll go ahead with the score.'

We reeled back over the ditch, laughing like loons. Our first excursion may well have been a cause for Confession for one poor soul but I had found friends.

After that the basement teas became less formal. I began to discover that the lads were reading the signs of the times and fretting for the future of the church.

'We have the whole week tied up in duties, for God's sake; Masses to be said, children to be christened, anointing the sick and burying the dead. I'm not taking from them; they're part of it too. But we should be doing less and listening more. It's going to pass us by. Mark my words, we're minding the shop instead of selling the goods.'

Indeed, the duties could very easily become a narcotic against thought. A full diary could give the illusion of a worthwhile service and these men were aware that busyness was a subtle and fatal temptation for any priest. With the oil still fresh on my forehead, I was blind to that. I immersed myself in First Fridays and Communion rounds, Confessions and Masses. The theology I had learned from the neck up was now being parsed into practice by the needs of the people. I began to realise that the demands on the priest challenged him to move from the head to the heart. To be 'in the world and not of it' was a scriptural slogan that had been overused to the point of cliché in our training. The people who were now becoming my tutors would never ask me for a theological explanation of original sin but they would draw me into involvement in their lives and loves, and face to face with what it meant to be a man who was also a man of God.

This was the beginning of my journey out of law and into love, and I had gifted guides. The elderly couple in Blarney Street sat side by side in the kitchen for Confession. When he saw my hesitation the old man smiled.

'Sure she knows all my sins anyway,' he said.

I began to grow accustomed to the fact that a twenty-year absence from the 'box' might need a few pints of stout to oil the cogs of repentance and that my job was to hold my breath and judgement as the heady odours of Murphy's brewery wafted through the grille; and that it was more important to comfort the child who had dropped the host on the floor than to fuss about how to raise the body of Christ from the dust. The bench outside my box was packed with penitents 'tryin' out de new fella'.

I remembered the story often told in the diocese of the parish priest who ruled alone and with a rod of iron. He was a tough confessor and would often exclaim loudly, 'You did what?' to the shame of the penitent and the entertainment of those wading through a long penance outside. Out of the blue, the bishop gifted him with a brand new curate, a round-faced, jolly boy who was as sweet-natured as his superior was sour. On Saturday night the tide of people ebbed from the parish priest's side of the church and overflowed the curate's benches.

After a time sitting inside the silent grille, the parish priest could contain himself no longer. He thrust his head out through the curtains and roared, 'Is there a slope in the floor or what?'

'Doc' Harte and I had a gentlemen's agreement never to discuss theology but privately I had him labelled as a conservative. Yet he was my faithful teacher and led me gently to the heart of the priesthood. Many's the time he said innocently, 'We'll go for a walk', and led me to to the kitchen of a widow who was obviously expecting us. There would be a fine cloth on the table and the good ware set ready. She would happily fuss over us for hours.

'Eat all that now, boy, and put a bit of weight on you; sure there's not a pick on you. Father, I often saw more fat on a grilled rasher.'

'Yerra, that fella has a hollow leg,' he'd say indulgently. And for those few hours we simply kept her company and gave her a reason to rise above her loneliness.

I remember the woman who helped me into my coat after one such visit.

'Wisha, God bless him,' she whispered at the door, 'but he takes me outta meself.'

He was an easy touch with an open pocket.

'God bless ye, Father, but I'm a bit short like.'

'That fella's making game of you,' I said irritably. 'Sure he'd drink out of a sore heel.'

'Wouldn't it be better to be taken for a fool than a miser,' he'd say gruffly.

He was shrewd enough to spot the danger signs of righteousness in his curate, so he sent me to take catechism classes in Eason's Hill school.

The school was tucked up a lane, the filling in an

ecumenical sandwich between Shandon and the cathedral. In deference to both persuasions, the pupils took the time from the four clocks of the former and religious instruction from the clergy of the latter.

'They'll knock the corners off ya,' he said with relish.

I remembered with a sinking heart the day a few years before, when he had cornered me into going with him on the school outing.

'We're going down to Father O'Leary's grave in Gougane Barra. It'll be great gas.'

They boiled onto the bus, laden down with bottles of Taylor Keith orange and bags of crisps. The first hiccup happened before the driver had time to let off the handbrake.

'Father, Tony can't go without his Mam.'

'Let her come,' he said cheerily.

'Father, I can't leave Mary at home.'

'The more the merrier,' he shouted, seemingly immune to the sounds and smells of raucous boys. I sat across the aisle from him, trying to maintain some clerical dignity, wondering uneasily if the character perched on the seat beside me had been to the toilet before we left.

We sailed down Roman Street with loud cheers and ribald comments from the windows. A line of mothers stood out at the doors waving with relief as we turned the North Infirmary and crossed the North Gate Bridge into the uncharted wastes of the Southside. The noise abated a little when we hit the Straight Road and ran out of houses.

'Jay, look, lads, fields!'

It was too good to last.

'Stop de bus, Mary's pukin'!'

I walked up and down beside the bus as Mary and a few sympathisers made their contribution to the environment, wondering if the Doc would notice if I made run for it. However, we screamed into Gougane Barra to the strains of their favourite song, 'McCarthy's Party':

'Twas at McCarthy's party
Everyone was hearty;
Someone knocked Maguire round de room
With the handle of a broom;
McCarthy and his cousin
Paralysed a half a dozen
Down at McCarthy's party.

The monastic quiet of Gougane Barra was soon ringing to happy shouts as they played hide-and-seek in the monks' cells. The more energetic waded into the holy well in search of treasure, or chipped the pennies from the pilgrims' cross. The teachers, Doc Harte and myself, took political asylum in the hotel for lunch, and a line of squashed faces followed every forkful from the windows.

'Father,' said the owner, 'will you come out and talk to them. They're chasin' the sheep.'

With a few bellows and the odd clip to the ear of an overenthusiastic sheep-chaser, Doc Harte got them into order for the photograph. They massed proudly on the flat slab of Father O'Leary's tomb and then we took the long sleepy road home. Of course there were the obligatory stops at convenient furze bushes, but finally I fell off the bus outside the presbytery, vowing, 'Never again!'

And now, like Daniel, I was being garnished in collar and new soutane and dispatched as a tasty morsel to the lions' den.

As I stepped into the hallway I heard a young fella call out, 'Lads, will ye look at Sandeman.'

It was a portent of doom if I needed one. The class was a disaster.

'Lads, God is like our father.'

'If He's like my oul' fella you can keep him.'

'Father, Father, Jimmy stuck his tongue out at me when he had Communion on it. Isn't that a mortal sin, Father?'

I began to wish I was a missionary so that I could distract them with stories of snakes in the sleeping bag and crocodiles in the bath, but that sort of adventure was rare enough in Kildare.

'Lads,' I shouted, in a moment of inspiration, 'we're going to have a play.'

'Hurray!'

'Can I be the oul' doll?'

'Now boys, did ye ever see a passion play?'

'Yeah, down behind Shandon on a Saturday night.'

'No, no, where do they have a passion play?'

One studious little fella raised a tentative hand. 'In Yobberamegum, Father.'

'Good man. So who wants to be Jesus?'

'Father! Father!' A forest of hands. I searched for the hand that wasn't there, working on the principle that he who is not for you is against you.

'Josser, you're just the man for the job.'

Josser was twelve going on thirty. His shirt opened all

the way down to his navel and his hair was watered back into a 'duck's ass', so tight it would make your eyes water. The props were simple enough.

'Where will we get the whips for the scourging?'

Two fellas disappeared out the classroom window and dispossessed two 'young wans' whipping tops in the lane.

'Now, what about the crown of thorns?'

This time the volunteer was gone a little longer and returned with a floral wreath.

'Where did you get that?'

'From the graveyard, Father.'

I had visions of clambering into the Protestant graveyard in my new soutane and explaining to the rector how I happened to have a wreath under my arm.

''Tis perfect.'

Josser's swagger began to slip a little at the whipping scene when the whippers became overenthusiastic. He started to growl ominously when the rabble pressed the wreath over his head.

'He's like de May procession.'

Finally he stood up on a chair with his hands outstretched for the crucifixion, flanked by two bickering small fellas on lower chairs.

'I'm de good teef, boy.'

'You are in me eye. I'm on de right side, see.'

'Oh yeah . . . '

'Now, lads,' I said, remembering long-ago drama courses on improvisation, 'you're the crowd and you must mock and taunt him.'

They were totally caught up in the play at this stage.

'Come down offa dat cross, ye knacker.'

'He was so smart healin' everyone else. You're a proper daw now, aren't ya!'

It was more than Josser could bear. With a roar, he was off the cross and had two Pharisees in a headlock before I could drag him off.

'You were magnificent, Josser.'

'Piece o' cake,' he said, sauntering back to his seat.

I crawled into the Doc's room on my hands and knees.

'Hail, the conquering hero!' he laughed.

'The divil rot your purple socks!'

'Will ya have a cuppa tea?'

'I'd prefer a pint of blood.'

I had to give him a blow-by-blow account and he laughed so hard I hoped he'd choke.

''Tis a long way from John the Evangelist,' he said between gasps, 'but 'twill make a man of you.'

I couldn't wait to tell Jim Keating, but a sick call came through from the North Infirmary and I had the oils in my pocket.

'In here, Father.' The nurse took me straight to casualty where the cardiac arrest team leant back so that I could anoint the elderly woman on the table. Then they jolted her again with electricity, lifting her body convulsively off the bed.

'Her son is in the waiting room, Father. Would you like to go out to him?'

In shock myself, I sat beside the young man until the doctor came through the swing doors and shook his head. 'I'm very sorry,' he said awkwardly, and moved away to the next case. The son began to cry and I sat beside him feeling inadequate, rubbing my hand between his shoulder blades until he stopped sobbing. It was what my father did for me whenever I had a nosebleed.

'I'll have to go and make the arrangements now,' he said, blowing his nose. 'And thanks very much, Father.'

I put my back against the wall outside on the street and tried to breathe. I had buried a mother, a grandmother and grandfather and a much-loved grandaunt, and had never come so close to seeing someone die. It took the heart out of me.

Jim read my face as soon as I walked in. 'Bridget, tea and loads of sugar.' I sat by the bed and began to tell him but the tears overtook me and I put my head down on the bed beside him. He stroked the back of my head with crooked fingers. 'You had a fright, boy; that's all right. Cry away now; sure what are you more than any man? 'Tis something you'll have to get used to.'

But I wanted to be more than any man. I wanted to be Christ Himself in all His passion, weeping blood through hands and feet, and not be crippled by the man I was. I wanted to be Damien of Molokai and Mother Theresa all rolled into one. I wanted to salve the agony of the world, to lose myself in prayer, to flare and burn and in some way appease this cruel God who stopped that woman's heart and stole away the mothers of small boys. How could I tell this saintly soul how much I raged at his disease and his acceptance of it? And how could I face the fear that one day, one awful day, I might 'get used to it'? I might climb into that protective shell where hurts can't come and priests don't cry and it's enough to do what must be done. And who would I be then?

3

LIMBO

One of the most famous of the Northside characters was known as the Rancher. He went from door to door with a box car, selling bundles of sticks for the fire, but his gait behind the box car was that of a prince. The story goes that he was scavenging for bits one day in Cork's biggest lumberyard, when he was confronted by the owner.

The Rancher saw himself as the equal of any man and won a new disciple when he started the conversation with, 'Tell me, Mr. Haughton, as one timber merchant to another . . . '

He believed in barter and would slam a bundle of sticks on Statia Cahill's counter in exchange for a *Cork Examiner*.

Very few Northsiders believed in buying anything directly, so when I said that I was interested in buying a car someone said they had a 'mark'. A 'mark', I discovered, was a fella who knew a fella who was doing a line with the sister of a fella who worked in a garage. In this Byzantine way, I came into possession of a black Morris Minor. It was the visible proof that Polyfilla could be driven. Maynooth had given me two degrees in almost seven years but neglected to teach me how to drive. The Doc took me for instructional spins and drove me into spacious fields so that I could 'have a go' at the wheel without decimating the parish. He was a devout coward. I got my brother-in-law to park the Morris at the presbytery and pretended it didn't exist, making all my calls on foot, until the sick call came from Clogheen.

Walking was out of the question, so, wearing the purple stole around my neck like the Red Baron's scarf, I climbed behind the wheel of the Morris. Through divine inspiration I got it started at the third try. What followed was a proof of God's existence and power. Shandon Street was busy at the best of times and shoppers tended to desert their cars rather than park them. This turned the steep hill into a slalom to test the skills of real drivers. Fourth was the only gear I was comfortable in and I roared away, weaving around trucks and prams and shawled women who shouted, 'Bad cess to ya!' in my wake. There was a hairpin turn into Blarney Street and the Morris took it on two wheels, making a noise of protesting rubber straight out of *Bullitt.*

I kept the pedal to the floor until I was in open country and watched for the boreen on the left as instructed by the flight crew before take-off. Again the Morris protested on the bend, but now I was barrelling down a narrow lane with grass growing in a line down the middle. The hysteria I had felt earlier was replaced by euphoria until I rounded the bend and there, before me, dead centre in the lane, was a big man in a helmet, dwarfing a small scooter. He was serenely putt-putting along, blissfully unaware that Fangio was racing for the chequered flag.

The Morris had one dud headlamp, and the steering wheel had the loosest of relationships with the wheels. More important still, the brakes were optional. As if in slow motion, I saw the look of serenity turn to surprise and then terror on the biker's face as we raced towards each other in a classic Mexican stand-off. Then he was doing the Wall of Death along the ditch, flying horizontally by the passenger window.

I ran back to where he was sitting on the verge, a bemused expression on his face as he watched his bike resting on its handlebars in the other ditch.

'Sorry about that. Are you all right?'

'N'yah,' he said.

'Ah, thank God. Am I right for Donovan's farmhouse?'

'N'yah,' he said again, nodding his head, a wavering finger pointing in the direction I was heading.

News travels fast. 'Doc,' I said when I got back to the presbytery, 'I think I'll take a few driving lessons.'

'Yerra, not at all, boy,' he said drily. 'You'll put the fear of God into more people with your driving than you ever will with your preaching.'

But the news everyone wanted to hear was where would the bishop appoint me.

Kevin gazed at the boiled egg with all the trepidation of Howard Carter at the threshold of Tutankhamun's tomb. He sighed as if the inevitable could be postponed no longer and tapped experimentally around the rim before cautiously lifting the cap.

'Soft,' he muttered darkly, 'again. I'd say Bantry,' he declared around the first mouthful.

'No way,' said Donovan, waving his arms for emphasis. Kevin shifted the milk jug out of range; a discussion with Donovan could be chronicled in the stains on the table-cloth.

'Schull,' he said, 'definitely Schull.'

They both laughed. In Maynooth the Cork students had their own croquet pitch. It was reasonably level except for one deep depression. To generations of Cork seminarians that hole was known as Schull. My laugh wasn't as hearty as theirs.

'Maybe he'll send you to Peru. Have you any Spanish, Christy?'

'*Un pocito.*'

I could see they were impressed by this, unaware of the fact that it had cost me half of my Spanish vocabulary. The diocese had adopted parishes in Peru some years before, and occasionally we saw photographs of the priests working there. The black-and-white pictures were usually posed before a blinding white wall, and because the lads wore white shirts, we saw two rows of black pants and two uneven rows of smiling faces. I remember sitting on the altar boys' bench as Father Michael Murphy spun yarns to the men's confraternity about the mission in Peru. Towser and I were engrossed in working out how far we'd have to edge down the bench before Falvey fell off. But I gathered that the Peruvians lived in galvanised houses like the ones we built in the quarry behind our houses.

'Of course,' the preacher said, 'the priests have to come down from the mountains to the coastal regions at regular intervals.'

'Das in case dey get de bends,' Towser remarked knowledgeably. 'Me Mam sez me uncle gets dem if he gets down too quick from the high stool in Flaherty's pub.' The bench nodded sagely. Schull began to look more appetising.

The neighbours weren't immune from speculating either.

'You might be sent out the country.'

Rose, our next-door neighbour, said this with an expression of horror. To Northsiders, civilisation paused at the North Gate Bridge and stopped dead at the city limits. 'The country' was lovely for a day out, but how could a body be expected to live there, 'miles from anyone'?

'You'll have to start watchin' *The Riordans* on the telly if you're sent out to the buffers,' Rose laughed. At the time, she was hugely pregnant and way overdue.

'Any move, Rose?'

'Yerra no, boy; sure he'll be talkin' back to me.'

I was sleeping next door in number six, still scaring myself at the sight of the black soutane looming on the wardrobe door in the morning. Some time during the night Rose nudged Jerry in the bed beside her.

'Jerry.'

'Wha'? Wha'?'

'The baby.'

'Wha'?'

'I think he's comin'.'

'Jesus!'

Jerry catapulted himself into the sleeping lane and ricocheted from door to door.

'Madgie, Norma, Eily, Mary, the baby's comin'.'

The men turned over as the women tumbled out. Swathed in dressing-gowns and prickly with curlers they gathered around Rose.

'I think the baby's comin'.'

'Oh, St Anthony,' Jerry prayed, 'what'll we do!'

'Never mind St Anthony, boy. Put on the kettle.'

'D'ye want tea?' the poor man asked in amazement.

'Ah lovin' God, Jerry, we need the hot water for the baby. D'ye know, there's an awful want in fellas.'

'Madge, what'll we do if the baby comes before the ambulance?'

'I think you pick them up by the ankles and slap their bottoms.'

'Go 'way!'

'On me soul, sure didn't you have your own?'

'Yerra, I was as high as a kite, girl. My fella said I was using language you wouldn't hear down the docks.'

They were stumped.

'D'ye know what,' said one, clutching her dressing-gown tighter for authority, 'we should send in next door for Christy Kenneally. They do a course in that class of thing.'

This was all the inducement the baby needed and he sensibly presented himself in the bed. Within minutes the fire-brigade ambulance was winking at the end of the lane and two large and jovial firemen were settling Rose on the stretcher.

'That's a grand cabinet, ma'am. Where did you buy it?'

'Jim Mack made that for me. Sure you'd swear it grew there!'

The house was suddenly silent and the women sat at the kitchen table, exhausted and slightly hysterical from the excitement. Jerry broached a bottle of brandy to 'steady me nerves' and they were persuaded to join him in christening the new arrival.

'I'll just wet me lips.'

'Mary, give us an oul' song.'

'Is it off your game ye are!'

'Ah go on, girl! Jerry, fill up her glass.'

Years before, in a plain black gymslip and scarlet sash, Mary stood on the stage at the Feis and swept the judge's table of silver with a voice of the same alloy. Now she straightened her back, tilted her bright face and sang:

Oh land of love and beauty
To thee our hearts we bring . . .

The women around her were no strangers to loss and hardship and now the lilt of the old song soothed their tired faces to a sweet serenity. Their gaze turned inwards in contemplation of other songs and other voices, long stilled in this world but echoing always in their hearts. In the absence of my mother I had tuned myself to voices such as theirs; voices that chided me in off the road from danger or into kitchens smelling of ironing for the 'baat' of bread and jam and a heat to the fire with their own. These were the faces that changed now with the mood of the song as the lane they lived in changed when clouds roved over the crack of sky between their roofs. I remember at parties and weddings nestling in their closeness as they honoured the 'noble call' or, tucked in bed, smelling of smoke and smuts on Bonfire Night, drifting away to their chorus from around the dying embers in the quarry. Now, as if to soothe the pain of the past and welcome the sign of the future, they rose to the chorus.

> When you cry we hear you;
> When you weep we weep.
> In your hour of gladness
> How our pulses beat.
> Ireland, mother Ireland,
> Let what may befall.
> Ever shall I hold you;
> Ever shall I hold you,
> Dearest, sweetest, best of all.

I was the boy who had 'gone away to the priesthood' and that night I did not hear their singing through the wall that divided us.

The second delivery of the day was waiting for me in the presbytery. The handwriting on the blue envelope was inimitable.

'I hereby appoint you as chaplain to St Patrick's Hospital in the Wellington Road.'

I wasn't going to Schull after all or 'out the country', or even to Peru. I was about to embark for a different world entirely.

4

THE INCURABLE

Someone said
The air had smelled of urine.
Their hollow coughing kept her from her sleep
And there are those
Who still must cross themselves
To hurry past the gates
But I had known
Their spittle on my fingers from the rounds,
Their secrets whisper-woven in my stole,
Their sometime laughs,
And time and time goodbyes.
Small wonder then that I still weep
Estranged from Paradise.

St Patrick's had always been a place people mentioned in whispers. Generations of Northsiders sprinkled their doorposts with holy water against the red-robed angel of tuberculosis, hoping, like the people of Israel, that the terror would pass them by. And when the dreadful coughing began and couldn't be contained, the shadows of their loved ones were finally 'shifted' to St Patrick's. Old memories die hard in our community and it was still common practice for people to go out of their way to avoid the iron gates or to bless themselves as they quickened their step on the Wellington Road. It was known as 'The Incurable'.

And it kept that name, long after TB had lost its lethal sting. Now it was the last resting place for those who carried incurable cancer. All of mine had died in Dublin or in the North Infirmary and I had only the vaguest idea where the hospice was. Growing up in the Northside meant knowing the web of streets and lanes that stretched to within a half-mile radius of home. Blarney Street, Grawn, Spangle Hill and Blackpool were home to some of the diaspora of people who had married out from the core. These were places we adventured to and got familiar with as we grew older. We organised outings to the pictures on the island between the two arms of the river, and that was 'Town'. Occasionally we went in formal procession across the river to my Nan and aunties in the Southside, always relaxing into familiarity as we recrossed the bridge into Shandon Street. I knew St Patrick's was somewhere on the hill above the railway station and below Montenotte. These were exotic places; to qualify for residency in Montenotte, the locals laughed, you had to have adenoids and money.

The reactions increased my apprehension. Jim solemnly folded the *Examiner*. 'You're very young for that,' he said quietly. My father reached across the oilcloth and squeezed my hand. He tried to say something and couldn't. Even the bishop seemed hesitant. Since my ordination he had been careful to use my formal title any time we met. Now he held my elbow at the door of the palace.

'You'll do your best, Christy?'

I followed the directions.

'Cross Patrick's Hill from Leitrim Street and you're on the Wellington Road. Christian Brothers College will be to your right and a high footpath to your left. Go up the hill till you strike a high wall. That's it.'

There was an iron gate set in the wall with an tidy apron of cobbles before it. The drive meandered left and then right through the garden to the front of the building. The hospital itself was a mixture of plain and fancy. It had a ruddy, honest face of Cork sandstone bordered with white limestone. This reminded me of the South Gate Bridge, which the locals claimed showed sandstone to the country side and limestone to the city side, for grandeur. I looked up from the bottom of the steps at three storeys, and down one to the basement. The windows were rimmed with yellow brick and, over to my right, a small balcony hung out from the top floor. A cluster of wheelchairs glinted in the sunlight, their occupants vivid in coloured shawls and blankets. A man in a wide straw hat waved tentatively. I waved back, just as cautiously. I felt like Gary Cooper in *High Noon*, totally outgunned and the sun in my eyes.

The first person I met inside the door was Pat, the receptionist, the only other male on the staff. TB had brought Pat to St Patrick's as a patient. Remarkably, he actually got better, to the consternation of the Sister, who had him measured for the habit and ready for a divine departure. He told me the story himself, punctuated with long, ruminative drags at the ever-present cigarette.

'She says to me, "Pat, I think you're not going to die." God, I felt like apologising. "Not yet, Sister," says I. "Maybe you'd get up," says she. "We need the bed." Lazarus was back from the tomb, boy, and nobody knew what to do with him. Well, to make a long story short, they needed someone to answer the phone and direct the visitors, so here I am.'

His kingdom was a small glass cubicle in the corner of the hallway. He had to fold his long legs almost into his armpits to squeeze inside, but every morning Pat travelled across the city on the Ballyphehane bus carrying a brown briefcase. The briefcase bore the tools of his trade: a carefully folded *Examiner* and a pair of brown felt slippers.

'I'm a martyr to me feet.'

He was standing now in his favourite position, the door behind him slightly ajar so that he could scan both ends of the corridor. The first fag of the day was already well under way, hanging from a pale, freckled hand.

'Noreen,' he said to a passing nurse, 'would you look at the child Connie sent up to us. I'd better send for Mamma.'

'Mamma', I discovered, was his code name for Reverend Mother, a tall, spare and serious lady who seemed to run on castors. She shunted me ahead of her into the gated lift and we ascended in an awkward silence to the top floor. The tour started there and spiralled back to the ground floor through the wards on each level. I noticed that the basement kitchen wasn't part of our itinerary.

My impressions were of long waxed corridors lined with portraits of the usual saintly suspects. High windows looked out on the terraced back gardens. The wards to the front of the building were spacious and bright, benefiting from the sun's passage across the city from Blackrock in the estuary to its red roost over the shoulder of Sunday's Well. White beds replicated each other down both sides of the wards. The nuns in charge shook hands briefly and fell into step as a guard of honour until we left their domain for the next ward. Mamma set a brisk pace but I saw men and women who smiled or nodded from beds or chairs, and some who hardly dented the bedclothes, their eyes locked on the faces of the young nurses who stroked their yellowed fingers. It took all of ten minutes to march me through my entire parish, and then at the door I was handed back to Pat, who would 'look after me'.

'Time to view the villa,' he said, smiling, when we were safely out on the steps. I paused by the railings, pretending to admire the view across the spiked spires of the city but guiltily gulping deep breaths of fresh air. No amount of disinfectant and air freshener can fully camouflage the smell of sickness and my stomach rolled dangerously. Pat, ever the diplomat, retied his perfectly tied laces until I was ready. Just then an apparition appeared around the gable-end and headed in our direction. She was a woman of indeterminate age, dressed in a nurse's uniform straight out of Gilbert and Sullivan.

'Pat, who's that?'

'That's Kathleen,' he said ominously.

'And what's that sample in front of her?' I asked, nodding towards a small hairy bundle that hoovered the ground before her at the end of a dog-lead.

'For the love and honour of God, Father dear, be careful. That mangy excuse for a dog is Dinky and he's the light of her life. For the sake of peace on earth, don't cross her.'

I was reared on terriers that earned their keep and our respect taking rabbits from the ditches of Nash's boreen and snapping rats in the small backyards off the lane. There was a small pink bow tied to the tuft of hair between this article's ears. It was all I could do to be civil.

'Lovely dog, ma'am.'

Kathleen seemed to inflate and glow. 'Dinky, say hello to the new priest.'

The sample and I regarded each other with mutual suspicion.

'Come on now, Dinky love, or we'll be late for our tea.'

Pat waited till she was well out of earshot.

'D'ye know,' he said, 'she was taking Dinky for his constitutional one evening and didn't she meet a fella walking a bitch of the same make. "D'ye know what, ma'am," says yer man, "maybe we could mate them."

'"What!" says Kathleen. "My dog was reared in a convent. He don't know nothing about them things."'

We passed a large statue of the Sacred Heart in the garden and it occurred to me that He was facing the wrong way, looking accusingly out over the docks with His back to the wards.

The villa was a felt-roofed flat tucked against the wall at the foot of the garden. We entered through a glass porch into a wide, carpeted living-room. I was transfixed by the open fireplace. Maynooth had never been warm enough and I think I got involved in dramatic productions because there was an open fire in the Green Room. Fuel for the fire posed a practical and a moral problem. The only turf available was neatly boxed outside the professors' doors. I've always thought that the soutane was a marvellous invention. Apart from giving ecclesiastical grace to the most ungainly of seminarians, it could also accommodate two briquettes in each pocket. Problem solved.

Off the long sitting-room were a kitchenette, bathroom and bedroom. To a fellow who had spent seven years in different single rooms, this was the Ritz.

'Pat, this is terrific.'

He looked out over the top of his glasses. ''Tis at the bottom of the garden up against a wall with a flat roof to catch the water. 'Tis a death trap.'

But even when my sisters sniffed suspiciously and an interesting green mould began to grow on my soutane, I could see no fault in it. This was home.

5

THE DAY

The old woman loved a love song:
'Sing "Sorrento"; course you know it
or "Sweet Mystery of Life".'
There's a song she'd sung by evening
Giving encore each new morning
In the hard-gloss hollow bedroom.
She was Callas, I Caruso
Till one night I said, 'Tomorrow,'
And she kissed my hands in parting.

The phone rang at 6.30 am.

'Good morning, Father. It's six thirty and a lovely morning.' The night matron was properly formal despite the weather forecast. When we got to know each other better she'd say, 'Get up outta that! The holy nuns have a half a day's prayin' behind them already.'

The little sacristy was dark with mahogany, spicy and warm with incense and beeswax. On weekdays I flew solo and would dive into the vestments and sit for a while in the armchair, trying to come awake or at least gather my thoughts for Mass. This was a slice of the day I grew to love, the time before anything started. It was a small circle of quiet away from the hustle and bustle, where the slow brown tick of the clock and the faint tap of rain on the roof combined to soothe me into stillness. I think it reminded me of the 'caboose' under the stairs at home, where I could curl up, alone and undisturbed. The bell shook me awake.

'In the name of the Father . . . '

At Sunday Mass I was shepherded by the Campbell brothers; rangy redheads, buttoned into sawn-off soutanes, uncomfortably clean in white surplices. Dave, steady and wry, was the elder of the duo. Frank was designed by a committee in disagreement, each of his legs on a separate contract. Dave spent half the Mass nudging me in the right direction and the other half anticipating Frank's disasters. While he was distracted one morning, Frank managed to miss the chalice and pour a whole cruet of wine up my sleeve. For a mad moment I was about to offer the other sleeve for the water. When he arrived with a fingerbowl and without the towel, I got a sweet revenge by drying my hands in his surplice. It nearly shocked him into coordination.

At the stroke of seven on weekdays I hit the altar at full throttle and was swept along through the Eucharistic mystery, buoyed up on the soprano responses of the Sisters counterpointed by the bass rumble of the Christian Brothers, who joined us each morning. At the end of Mass I took the full ciborium and set out for the wards, one of the Sisters walking ahead of me with a small warning bell and a lighted candle that pushed the shadows before us.

'The Body of Christ. Amen.'

Those who were able sat up in their beds, the women with shawls around their shoulders, their faces stretched from the facecloth, composed and stiff. The men always reminded me of how Pop would receive Communion. I remember his stillness when the priest approached and how he'd raise his head and give a little nod, as if to acknowledge a friend. He looked as vulnerable as a child when he put out his tongue for the wafer. Then he'd return to his seat, slowly and distractedly, as if he were carrying on a conversation with himself. I learned to read the nods and signals of the nurses who hovered in the shadows near the beds of those particularly low, and sometimes broke a host to place a tiny fragment on a dry, swollen tongue.

It often happened that someone was too weak to receive and I remembered something I had started to do instinctively while I was in the cathedral. Parents often brought small children with them to the rails and, to pre-empt a premature First Holy Communion, placed a hand over the child's mouth as they themselves received. I was often confronted by a parent with eyes shut and mouth open, and their gagged image and likeness glaring at me in indignation. So I began to put my hand on their heads briefly in blessing. This became my practice in my new parish among people whose sickness had already excluded them from so much.

Breakfast was served by Marie in the chaplain's dining-room. She staggered in under a tray that could have fed Collins Barracks.

'Marie, I'll never manage that.'

'You will, Father,' she said pleasantly.

Another legacy of Maynooth was a shrunken stomach.

'I won't, Marie.'

She evaporated in confusion, to be replaced by a Sister from below, her sleeves rolled for combat, her face shiny with determination.

'Will you not ate your breakfast?'

'I couldn't manage it, Sister, but I'd love an egg.'

'An egg. Sure you couldn't live on that.'

'Well, maybe a bit of toast with it. That would be grand.'

A plump chaplain was a source of pride. I was a great disappointment to them.

So here I was, twenty-five years old and I had never seen anyone die. I had managed to go through seven years of training without a single lecture on how to be a hospital chaplain. What to do? From the time I first learned to read, I found a world of answers and escape in books. There had to be a book somewhere that would tell me what to say and who to be. It was time to go to Egan's.

In Cork at that time there were shops and stores and Egan's was neither. It was an establishment. The two windows fronting on Patrick's Street were ambivalent in their dedication to God and Mammon. One side glittered with expensive silver plate and the other shone with chalices and cloth of gold. The lower floor was an Aladdin's cave of light-filled cabinets, groaning under the weight of potential wedding presents, trophies and silver salvers. The walls were studded with clocks that tocked in time to my footsteps on the polished floor. A broad staircase swept upwards and divided. Whichever route took your fancy, you fell under the benign gaze of Tom, a smooth, smiling Buddha, who had the soft, hushed voice of a librarian. The bookshop itself was a large high-ceilinged room, a treasure-trove of titles. Where else in Cork could you find a slim, erotic D. H. Lawrence cheek by jowl with the stolid Hans Küng? Where would you find P. G. Wodehouse, chirping lightly about the unflappable Jeeves, or Heinrich Böll describing someone as 'having the eyes of a cardinal who had lost the faith'? It was a place where time stood still, and I often had to run the Wellington Road to deliver a sweaty Benediction.

It was here, as I expected, that I found the answer to my prayers. Elisabeth Kubler-Ross was a Swiss GP who had a Pauline conversion to the care of the dying patient. Almost singlehandedly she had dragged her profession out of the trance of technology to consider the needs of those for whom 'no more could be done'. More important still, she had distilled all the answers to my questions into one slim volume. Dan, a former Glen hurler and therefore a member of the extended family, took my bundle at the register.

'How are you getting on above, boy?'

'Fine, Dan.'

He was always happier with round figures.

'We'll say a fiver.'

A visitor once asked Pop if I was fond of the books.

'Fond of them? He ates them, boy,' he answered proudly.

I devoured that book, underlining passages in biro and

scribbling notes in the margins until I could recite some pages by heart. I was now the world's living expert on the stages of dying and could trip them off my tongue from denial to acceptance, like a child answering his catechism question and with about the same level of comprehension.

Ah, pride! I had forgotten the famous words of our ecclesiastical history professor in Maynooth. This man would often quote Dante in Italian as if we should know it and stare in mock horror at our blank expressions. One particular day he leant dolefully over the podium and declared, 'Look at them. All of them reading about life and none of them living it.'

We thought it was hilarious. The following morning I was to discover just how cruelly prophetic his words could be.

'Father, Sadie on the top floor wants to see you.'

I was suspicious of the suppressed smiles on the faces of the two nurses waiting at the door.

'We'll take you in to her, Father.'

There was a bump in the bed and no sign of Sadie.

'He's here now, love.'

The bump moved and Sadie's grey head rose like a periscope from the depths of the blankets. 'Ah, sweetheart,' she trilled in a high girlish voice.

I tried to ignore the giggles behind me and concentrate on Elisabeth Kubler-Ross. My mind was a complete blank. My Swiss guru was off eating Toblerone in some other dimension and I was marooned with Sadie.

'Will you do something for me, darling?' she cooed.

'Anything at all,' I answered manfully.

'Will you sing a song?'

Elisabeth Kubler-Ross came rushing back to me, chapter and verse, and there was not a single solitary reference to singing a song for the terminally ill. Even worse, I recalled that whenever I sang at home my father would laugh and say, 'Will you stand out at the front door so the neighbours will see we're not bating you.' At this stage the two helpful hussies were out in the corridor, hugging each other for support, breathless with laughter.

'What kind of song would you like, Sadie?' I said, stalling for time.

'A love song,' she said dramatically, 'always a love song.'

Most of my generation grew up giggling through the songs of aunts and uncles at family parties. Subconsciously, I suppose, we must have learned the words and airs of hundreds of old songs. 'Ah, sweet mystery of life at last I've found you,' I began. I could hear one of them coughing outside.

May she choke, I thought savagely.

Sadie turned her head sideways on the pillow, her milky eyes questing away from the here and now in search of happier times.

'Now at last I know the secret of it all.'

She nodded sadly at that line then joined me in a high, cracked voice for the rest of the verse:

All the longing, seeking, striving, waiting, yearning,
The burning hope, the joy and idle tears that fall;
For 'tis love and love alone the world is seeking;
For 'tis love and love alone that can repay.

As we moved to the final line I sat beside her and her withered hand stole into mine:

Now the answer, 'tis the end and all of living
For it is love alone that rules for aye.

In the sudden silence she raised my hand gently to dry, feathery lips.

'Thank you,' she squeaked, and submerged again under the blankets.

As the days went by, I looked forward to the crazy concerts with Sadie. Many's the time I dragged reluctantly up the stairs, freighted with the worry of a child in school or a dark tale from the 'box' or just the emptiness of the flat, and found solace with Sadie. She never allowed any change in the programme. Theology, philosophy or any talk of death were strictly off limits – the song was all. Gradually I forgot all about the stages of dying and Sadie's progress towards acceptance, until one morning Pat called me into the cubicle on my way to the boiled egg.

'They want you for Sadie.'

'Sure I only anointed her lately.'

'She won't do, boy,' he said gently.

I took the stairs at a run, angry with myself for letting Sadie 'sell me a pup'. My job was to steer her through the stages of dying, get her habit on, hands crossed, have her pointed east and ready for take-off. Then I would have done my job; then I could mark my internal scorecard with a tick against Sadie's name, yet another one notched up for God.

This time her head didn't rise, so I knelt near her and

shifted the blanket so she'd see my face. She came back from a distance to focus on me, as if I had called her.

'Ah, darling,' she said in a tired whisper, 'just in time for a song.'

There was one song I had studiously avoided during all our concerts. It was my father's song for his dead Maura, a pledge of love and loyalty he was true to forever. Yet now, without thinking, I began to sing, 'We are in love with you, my heart and I.' I was kneeling on the lino, holding her hand in mine, and when I finished she raised my hand to her lips as always.

'Goodbye darling,' she said, 'and thank you.'

The business of the day swept me away from her room and it was at the Communion round early the next morning that I discovered her empty bed. I was rooted to the floor. The Sister turned with the candle and came back to me. 'She left us during the night, Father,' she said, and went back to stand guard outside the door while the chaplain sat on Sadie's bed and scrubbed his face with the hem of his stole. Sadie had gone to better things, where she could have her pick of Gigli, Caruso or Mario Lanza to sing her love songs. And she had left me something precious. I realised my job was to accompany the dying on their own private pilgrimage and not to push them along some route of my own. There was no book and never would be one that could teach me what to say or do. The heart would do the right thing if I wasn't too afraid to let it.

The little bell tinkled from the corridor, calling me back.

6

BEING THERE

The pools that were her eyes
flowed ever fuller in her face
as life began to ebb.
The plumb-line of our talk
no longer snagged
on the trivial flotsam of our lives
but daily deepened
till the line was taut and spent,
and words refused to measure more.
So, taking off my shoes
I paddled in the shadows of her room
or schoolboy-skimmed the pebbles of my prayers
across her pain.
And, for my effort
she would ripple me a smile
that lapped around my heart
and splashed my eyes.
I watched her for a month or more
I watched her thrash the seine of binding sheets
until she rose majestic on the waves

and left me silent on the shore,
bereaved.

When I was a child, nuns were the people who chased us out of the convent garden as we waded through cabbages in search of a submerged ball. Later there was Sister Eucharia, my teacher in school, who hassled and hugged us with equal passion, so that we vied to be her pet. While I was in secondary school, a pal of mine decided she wanted to become a nun. She was a bright, life-loving girl with an infectious laugh, and I wondered if that life would change her. She turned out to be dafter than ever, a Northside Maria Von Trapp, who could never manage to 'walk, Sister, walk'.

Maynooth admitted nuns to our lecture halls and they became so familiar as to be invisible. In the final year the custom was to get a photograph of everyone who had ever been part of the class and bequeath it to the college wall. Some fellas got a 'rush of blood to the head' and thought it inappropriate that the Sisters should hang with the rest of us. At a noisy meeting they threatened to stay out of the frame if the nuns got in. The nuns smile down from the wall to this day. The objectors don't feature. We thought of ourselves as liberal young men of the new church, and yet old stereotypes die hard.

I remember I had a part in a college play and some of the lads took a bra from the costume hamper and snuck it into my laundry bag. The laundry went out once a week to the convent outside the village. As soon as the van left the gates the plotters revealed the deed. I was in a sweat, waiting for an outraged letter from the Sister-in-charge to laundry number 254, or worse, an ominous nod from the dean. 'Mr Kenneally, an object of lady's apparel, etc.' When the laundry returned I found the contentious article neatly laundered and folded with all the other unmention-ables. There was a short note pinned to the bag, signed by the Sister-in-charge: 'We hope you'll both be very happy.'

And yet, when a nun came to die, I wasn't sure how I would relate to her.

'How are you, Sister?'

'I'm afraid,' she said simply. I was so shocked that she laughed.

'Well, that makes two of us, Sister. So, what will we do?'

'We'll see,' she said.

She made all the running herself. Some days we talked about something in the news and other days we talked about ourselves, swapping the kind of small childhood stories that people place in the foundation of what might become a friendship. Occasionally I brought her the gossip from the streets, stretching chords of contact to the world beyond the walls. As time passed I grew more comfortable with sitting in her silences, just keeping her company.

'D'ye know,' she said one day, 'you've never offered to pray with me?'

'No,' I said. 'I knew a chaplain once who didn't know what to say. He got more and more uneasy with the silence so he said to the man in the bed, "Will I pray with you?"'

'And what happened?'

'The man said, "Yes, if it helps you, Father."'

She began to laugh until the tears streamed down her cheeks. Then she coughed and fought for breath as blood appeared on her lips.

'Nurse, nurse!'

'No, no, I'm grand now.'

She took the tissue from me and dabbed her mouth.

'Would you like me to leave now?'

'No. I'd like you to pray with me.'

I'd been saying prayers since I could talk. I was most comfortable with the tried and trusted, and very wary of the scary ones in the ritual that were heavy on guilt, like the small print on a certificate for fire insurance. I had no book now and I was afraid. As a child I had prayed really hard that my Mam would come back and that Pop and Nan wouldn't die. She didn't and they did. My success rate was poor. But I knew she wasn't asking for an 'asking' prayer. We both knew that she would die, and soon. And so, with great trepidation, I stepped into unscripted waters, simply thanking God for being with us in the stories and the laughs and the silences. And then I was silent.

'Are you asleep?'

'No, but I think I can now.'

It was the last time we spoke. As she sank lower and her face took the colour of the bedsheets, the nurses were anxious that we should go through the rituals.

'Will you anoint her, Father?'

'No, I don't think she'd want that.'

They brought the candles and the crucifix anyway but I persuaded them that it would be better if I sat where she could see me when she woke. Occasionally she did wake and her eyes would fasten on me. I resisted the urge to take her hand, sensing that she was a very private person and that it would not be a comfort to her. But I broke our agreement not to ask God for something. I asked Him to let her die; she had suffered enough.

At some time on a spring afternoon, when the light threw lace patterns on the wall and the curtain swayed with the breeze from the open window, she stopped breathing.

7

MIRACLES

The countryman had put his trust
In the strong, wrist-hitch of harness,
Hup and heave of haybales
Plough-lined corduroy of an Autumn field.
The cancer on his lip
Could not be burnt like gorse
Or blasted, like the tumours on his land.
With every passing day,
The weed moved deeper in the man
And parasitic, sapped the manhood from his eyes
It brought him to despise his patch of clay.
The head, bent low between the shoulder-shafts,
Bent lower into shadow every day.
'I'm God's obscenity,'
He seemed to say.
The city girls were ignorant of blight
That rotted all things growing in the ground
But, wise to deeper things, they nursed the heart
And when he looked them in the eye
A man looked back.

They gentled him to live a second spring
His eyes were full of blossom
When he died.

I didn't believe in miracles.

How could God save me and lose you, and how did He decide? The picture of the Almighty sticking a pin in the paper, like my aunts did for the Grand National, didn't appeal to me, any more than soliciting the help of some heavenly TD to put a word in the right ear. But miracles do happen in the everyday and we had one.

Tom came in an ambulance without a siren. There was no rush; Tom was someone who couldn't be saved. He was a farmer who had ignored the lump on his lip until the mirror scared him into hospital. By then it was too late. They cut away a chunk of his lower face, swaddled him in bandages and sent him to us to die. As it happened, Tom had gone into remission, that limbo time when a cancer just stops developing. People stay in remission for different periods of time and it looked like Tom could stay there indefinitely. But he was suffering from a second illness, a kind of cancer of the soul, brought on by disgust at his own appearance. He hid his head on the way from the ambulance and, as soon as the bed was ready, he made a little tent of the blankets and crawled inside. At first I was never sure which end of him I was talking to. For my pains I got the odd grunt from the tent and gradually my talk petered out. I began to invent good excuses to visit other patients more often. This was always a great temptation. There was satisfaction in getting feedback from someone who wanted to talk and

I succumbed to it. Now I only met him on the ritual rounds for Communion or anointing. And then, the miracle happened.

Two 'young wans' from the Lower Road had a notion that they'd like to be nurses and were given summer jobs as aides on Tom's ward. They were as 'scattered' as their age entitled them to be and rarely out of trouble. But it was obvious to all that they had heart in abundance. However it happened, they were put in charge of Tom, looking after his small needs, and these included washing his face. I was at the door of the ward one day when they started with the facecloth. Tom kept his hand clenched firmly over the bottom half of his face and his eyes locked into the middle distance. The two teenagers talked easily about dances and fellas: who'd pay your way into a dance and who'd meet you inside.

'Yerra, that fella would buy you a bottle of orange at the dance and try and turn you into a cocktail-shaker on the way home.'

And all the time their hands moved gently with the cloth as if they were distractedly washing the jammy face of a well-loved child. He was looking from one to the other, amazed, I think, at the ordinary way they looked at him. Then, heartened by the warmth of their young hearts, his hand unclenched and left his face to rest easily on the bedclothes. Because two 'young wans' had given him back the gift of himself, he would never cover his face again.

As I stood in the doorway I began to realise that I had been intent on serving only half my parish. I had neglected the staff, especially the night staff, those women who came with sleepy eyes in the morning and the ones who worked below ground in the kitchen. I was a flat stone skimmed by a child across the surface of a pond. I could barely touch the patients' lives. These were the people who were with them all day, every day. It was time to ordain the staff.

I decided to start underground and work my way up.

We lived in a two-up, two-down house in Convent Place. It would be more accurate to say that we lived in one room. The 'front room' had the radio, the good table and the glass-case. It was for visitors and special occasions when we could sit before the fire in pyjamas making striped toast at the grate. We lived in the kitchen. The first time I ventured below ground to the hospital kitchen there was consternation.

'Was there something wrong with the breakfast? Did Marie forget a tray?'

'No, Sister, I came down to have a cup of tea with yourselves on your break.'

Sisters Salome and Sabina were probably named by some novice mistress with a grudge, but they were hard-working and sensible women who surfaced for Mass in the morning and submerged for the rest of the day in the steaming kitchen. What light there was in the kitchen emanated from themselves, because they made light of their lot and made much of the girls who worked with them. After the first fairly formal reception, they got used to me and stopped the vain search for a 'good' cup among the mugs in the cupboard. I noticed how they looked over my shoulder when I arrived, as if anxious that Mamma might be hovering behind me. Mamma, I was to learn, held the strong belief that all things had their proper place, including the chaplain. Occasionally, around a mouthful of Fig Roll, I painted pen pictures of the men and women in the beds above.

'John is low today but Suzy is a lot brighter.'

One day I surprised them by asking for their prayers. Most of the kitchen girls were from County Limerick and weren't shy about coming forward.

'Our prayers,' the redhead from Rathkeale laughed. 'Yerra, I prayed me oul' fella's greyhound would win the coursing and he's still runnin'. He says he's goin' to take him for a long walk out the country and run away from him.'

The two Sisters exploded with laughter before their sense of decorum could kick in.

'Sure, Father, we don't get time to pray. 'Tis different for the nuns on the wards. They can be over and back all day to the chapel once they're covered.'

'Well,' I said, 'my Nan was always up to her elbows in flour and suds. She said she hadn't time to be sick; didn't she inherit the four of us when my mother died.'

'God rest her soul,' they chorused.

'Anyway, I'd say I learned more from my Nan about prayer than I did in seven years in Maynooth.'

This had a whiff of heresy about it and they were hooked.

'How's that, Father?'

'Well, everything she did was a prayer because she did it for the love of us, and I feel the benefit of her prayers to this day.'

'What will we pray for?'

'Pray for me,' I said, "cos, to be honest with ye, there's days when I don't know what to do for the ones in the beds.'

They were aghast. How could a priest need prayers? But there were nights when I called on the power of the kitchen to see me through the watch with someone who was dying hard. They never failed me. I also believe they saved my life.

I preached a short sermon that particular Sunday, mindful of the journey before me. Fergus, my classmate, wanted me in Galway to help him pour water on his newest nephew. It would be a chance to renew our friendship and to experience that special affection parents have for a priest-son's friend. It was a perfect day, bright with promise, as I left the familiar closeness of Blackpool and blessed myself at the signpost for Whitechurch cemetery. Did that simple sign alert the dead? The Mallow road was only twenty miles long but it boasted over 108 bends. At one of them I struck the shoulder and felt the car go over. There was a huge grinding noise and then I heard the birds pick up their song uncertainly, as if disturbed at their Matins.

I was lying in a field with a perfect view of the mangled wreck that had been my car now beached upside-down beside me. Arms and legs moved; no pain. Standing, I tugged my shirt out of my trousers, and the windscreen, a shower of diamonds, fell around my feet. Two men stood on the ditch.

'Oh Jesus, 'tis a priest. Are you all right, Father?'

I saw ashen faces and felt eager hands.

'The top button is gone out of my shirt,' I said.

I was in someone's kitchen, sipping strong tea served by a fraught woman. Two children stared at me from solemn faces, the smaller one moustached with milk.

'Yes, I'm fine. I'm home now. Thanks very much.'

The two Samaritans drove off. I was in the kitchen.

'Father?'

'Have you any brandy, Sister? I'm not hurt, but I'll go down now for a rest.'

'Yes, Father.'

The doctor arrived at the villa in a flurry of nuns. The visible evidence was sparse – two bruised knees from the steering wheel and a bruised shoulder from my exit through the door.

'Someone must have been praying for you, Father,' he said wryly, shaking his head. How could I explain that the prayers of two kitchen Sisters, combined with those transferred from a slow greyhound in Rathkeale, had plucked the chaplain from an early grave? The stethoscope might have moved from heart to head. And how could I admit it to myself and not be challenged at the core of my beliefs?

Their sisters in the dark were the night staff. Many were married women who tucked their children in and left their sleeping houses to watch the night in St Patrick's. I wandered up around midnight and found the door locked solid. The bell jangled unmercifully. Tentative footsteps sounded inside.

'Who is it?'

''Tis me, the chaplain.'

Bolts rattled and keys turned.

''Tis easier to get into Fort Knox,' I said pleasantly.

The night nurse looked uncertain. 'Were you sent for, Father?'

'No, nurse, I just want to spend some time with the night staff.'

Her expression suggested disapproval and she disappeared towards her office on the ground floor. I hared up the stairs, suspecting she would be on the phone to warn the troops. The long black soutane was a mistake. Halfway down the dim corridor a nurse sailed backwards from a ward, balancing a tray of medications.

'Good night, nurse.'

'Oh Jesus. Well God forgive you, Father, but you took the heart out of me.'

''Twas one way to get you down on your knees,' I said, as we hunted on all fours after rolling tablets.

'For God's sake, will you leave that black yoke off you when you come up or the girls will think the place is haunted.'

It was a sound lesson in appropriate liturgical dress.

Everything was different at night. All the hubbub of the day, the rattle of trolleys and the clatter of heels were gone. The low lights smudged the high ceilings with shadows while, here and there, a night-light lapped devotedly at a saint's plaster toes. The sleeping forms around me hushed my voice, smoothed and oiled my movements as I walked between the beds.

'Is that you, Father?'

''Tis, John. Can you not sleep?'

'No, I find the night very long.'

'Mary was in tonight?'

'She was. She never misses. 'Tis hard on her, Father.'

This was often the prelude to a conversation or revelation that rarely braved the light of day. But we were two castaways sitting on a raft-bed, adrift on a sleeping sea. For an hour or so I could step from raft to raft with a small gift of words to pay my passage, or simply sit and stroke a hand or cheek with a tenderness I was shy of showing by day.

'Is there anything that helps you during the night, John?'

'There is, Father. I do see that small light at the bottom of the ward, where the nurse sits. That gives me great heart, 'cos I know she's there, like.'

I took that message to the tea-circle in the alcove off the ward, to emphasise the influence they had if they could be open to what the dark might offer.

Tess moved seamlessly in and out of reality but tonight she was wide awake and shaking.

'What is it, Tess?'

'Oh, Father. I'm in dread of me life.'

'Of what, girl?'

'Father, if a man got up to that window there – ' She paused for dramatic effect. ' – and got in,' she added darkly.

'Tess, there are three floors under us and bars on all the windows. Any man who could climb in that window deserves whatever he can get.'

Her eyes were like saucers with shock.

'God, you're a terror,' she said happily and lay back to sleep.

My last call was always to the blind woman.

''Tis me.'

'I know your step.'

The skin of her face was stretched from questing after sounds, but her hands could see. I grew accustomed to the way she'd raise them up to read my face, finding and kneading the cleft between my eyes with rough affection, like Nan and Dad did whenever I was sick at night and scared. Her fingers drew the tension from my day so that I could face the bed, a little less afraid of all the phantoms I had gathered on my rounds.

'Mamma's on the prowl.' Pat was as cryptic as ever. 'Were you up to any blackguardin'?'

'No more than usual.'

He rolled his eyes theatrically.

'Storm force ten, batten down the hatches,' he said gaily, curling his long legs into the cubicle. I hadn't long to wait. I had just decapitated the boiled egg when the formal tap sounded on the door.

'Come in.'

'Good morning, Father.'

'Good morning, Mother.'

I turned the knob of the radio and Terry Wogan beat a hasty retreat. He was well out of it.

'Wasn't that a very interesting reading at Mass this morning, Father?'

'Oh, which one was that, Mother?' I hedged, drawing a

complete blank in my memory of either.

'The first one, from the Old Testament, about Noah. Wasn't it wonderful how he took two of every creature into the ark?'

'Yerra, that's only a myth, Mother.'

There was the kind of silence that had occurred in the kitchen at home the day I asked Mary Ann what had happened her nose.

'A myth, Mother. Ye know, a story to get across some truth or revelation to the listeners,' I added lamely.

''Tis the inspired word of God, Father,' she said with great deliberation.

Suddenly the boiled egg assumed massive importance as I mined the yolk with a surgeon's precision.

'I understand you visit the wards at night, Father.'

The ferret was in the ditch now for certain. I laid the spoon aside and returned her gaze.

'I do, Mother.'

'Why?'

'To visit the patients who are awake and the night staff.'

'You didn't ask my permission.'

I was brought up to be that most peaceful and dangerous of creatures, the nice child. The nice child always says and does what is expected. The nice child goes to visit relatives and sits quietly for hours while they exclude him from the conversation. The nice child says 'Sorry' when he hasn't done anything wrong and smiles when he wants to scream.

'I don't actually need your permission, Mother.'

The breath hitched in my throat but I continued.

'Maybe I should have mentioned it to you first, out of

good manners, but I didn't think of doing so and I apologise for that.'

She nodded slightly.

'Do you intend to continue visiting the wards at night?'

'Yes, I do. Whenever I'm able.'

She stood up. 'Good morning, Father.' The interview was over and I was trembling.

Pat's head snaked around the door before I could draw breath. 'Will I send for O'Connor's undertakers?'

'A bit soon for that, Pat,' I said wanly.

He sat on her empty chair as I got a cup and saucer from the press and put them before him, annoyed at the rattle.

'I'd say she took Machiavelli for her Confirmation name. I don't trust her.'

Pat had the last word. 'And she doesn't trust you either, boy. No, don't be gettin' up on your high horse. Christy boy, you're young and you have all these new notions about the patients and the staff.'

'But, Pat . . . '

'Didn't I tell you to shut up and hear me out. If that woman stabs you it'll be in the front and then she'll offer you a cup of tea. Sure there's no understanding them. Anyway, 'twill be all the one to the worm.'

He was right. We had many battles, Mamma and I, and she never once sulked or carried a grudge. And years later when I walked into a hospice in Scotland where she was retired in exile and introduced her to my wife, she kissed me on the cheek. 'Ah, Christy,' she said, with a mischievous glint in her eye, 'as boyish as ever.' And I was glad to see her.

8

BACK TO SCHOOL

I was beginning to find my bearings without a map on a scrap of paper. I could navigate confidently from Camillus's through Patrick's to Anne's. I could even manage to operate the lift on my own and only very rarely make a grand exit from a ward into a brush cupboard. Like Alexander the Great, I was beginning to feel I had no more worlds to conquer. The blue envelope was leaning casually against the boiled egg and the sight of it brought me out in hives. Surely the bishop wasn't moving me just when I was getting the hang of things.

Chaplaincies like mine were sometimes seen by the higher powers as a handy base from which you could go out to work somewhere else. Once you had the Mass behind you and a few anointings done, sure what would you be doing with the rest of your time? It was a bit like the old story of the parish priest who was asked to recount his day. 'Arrah,' he said, 'I say Mass and a few prayers. I read the paper and have the breakfast. And then I slacken off a bit for the rest of the day.'

It was a shock to discover that himself was appointing

me as chaplain to five of the secondary schools in the city.

On Monday morning I adjusted my GAA and Northside prejudices to present myself at Presentation College on the Western Road. Brother Jerome, the principal, was larger than life and generous with the surplus. He was a glowing powerhouse of enthusiasm, radiating energy so that his cassock seemed to strain at the seams, and only the bellyband saved us all from an explosion. A priest I knew had said about him, 'You'd have to change your shirt after talking to that man.'

He whirled me through the introductions in the staff-room, then slapped me on the back. 'Go for gold, boy.' The staffroom flooded and ebbed with flying black togas at bell-marked intervals. Teachers rushed in for a cuppa, a mouthful of biscuit, a mound of copies, and then stormed off again. I was dizzy at the comings and goings, but the mid-morning break was an entertainment. Dan Donovan could have the place in roars as he moved like a chameleon from Shakespeare to what the huckster said in the Coal Quay.

'She decided to go upmarket from fish to lobsters and, of course, they were alive and racing around under the pram. She was down on her knees chasin' them when a Montenotte voice said, "Are they fresh?"

'"Well," says she, "I'm not windin' em up."'

I remember Jim Corr, kindly and solicitous, making the introductions and nudging me quietly into the circles of conversation. We decided that the best use of my time was to preside at class Masses, which were always held in the Sacred Heart Missionaries chapel at the head of the dyke. A young teacher called Hugh was charged with shepherding the group of reluctant Christians to the church without losing a few souls along the way to the wide open spaces of Fitzgerald's Park.

Some of the Sacred Heart Missionaries were around my own age, and one in particular was a dyed-in-the-wool devout support of St Finbarr's Hurling Club. All my crowd were rabid Glen Rovers followers. Uncle Joe had played with Ring and Jack Lynch in the banded jersey, and after him my brother Michael picked up the mantle and carried it with pride until he emigrated to America. Even I had managed to pick up senior and minor county medals with the club, more by accident than ability. Battle was joined, but in typical Cork fashion the 'slaggin'' and 'ball-hopping' were a camouflage for the genuine admiration and affection that existed between both camps. The Eucharistic Procession match was due, and it was usually a holocaust when these two were competitors. The bishop always threw in the ball to start the game and then had the good sense to sprint for the sideline out of the way.

'I suppose Connie will throw the ball to Jackie Daly, like he did last year? Ye have him well-trained.'

'He will, boy, but he'd better anoint Doolin first.'

In the hospital I could go for weeks on end without meeting another priest. This casual contact with a group of priests was very precious. One of their gifts was that they never took themselves too seriously. They told me one day of one of their members who liked to extend his influence to some of the city pubs on a Saturday night. He was wont to come home under the same influence, but when he boarded the bus he would announce in a loud voice that he wanted to be let off at the African Missions

House. At the designated stop he would be assisted to the pavement by the conductor and bid all in the bus a warm goodnight. Then, having ruined the reputation of that innocent order, he would weave the half mile back along the road to his own.

Now that I was 'back to school' I began to learn valuable lessons from the teachers.

Eamonn Young came to teaching as an afterthought. He brought with him to Bishopstown School all the man-management savvy he had gleaned as an army commandant, and a passion for his subject that took him out of the army and into the Uni. I learned from Eamonn that even the laziest pupil can't resist a teacher in love with his subject.

The first-year class in Douglas school came to a class Mass, perfectly tutored in the responses, which they roared back at me. I tried dropping my voice to tempt them into lowering theirs, but they roared even louder as if to encourage me. They had prepared their own prayers of petition and these were a lurid litany of requests.

'For me Nanny, 'cos she had her leg off. Eh, above the knee. Lord hear us.'

'Lord graciously hear us,' they thundered.

Brother Bede in Turner's Cross pulled out all the stops with themes and posters and readings they could pick from any source. He encouraged the lads to mine their own music for lyrics that were meaningful to their own lives. In short order we waded through the entire libretto of *Jesus Christ Superstar*. Jarlath, a retired and saintly Brother, always knelt at the back at these Masses to show solidarity with the boys. The poor man had to endure endless readings from *Jonathan Livingstone Seagull* and *The Little Prince* but his martyrdom was highlighted when they struck into a song about Vincent Van Gogh and sang, 'How you suffered for your sanity'.

Mayfield was special. They were starting with a brand new school and wisely determined to build from the bottom up. John, the principal, was a smiling man who shrewdly built up the morale of the staff while he built his school. Apart from himself and Dan, the vice-principal, I was a senior statesman and the only religious in a group of young, vibrant teachers. Already a local cleric had sounded off from the pulpit about the setting up of 'a godless college', but the local parents placed their faith and their children in the new community school. Any clerical affectation was soon kicked out of me in five-a-side soccer tournaments. But my visa into acceptance was stamped definitively the day I opened the tin at the break. Sister Sabina fretted at the idea that I wouldn't be back for the lunch.

'You'll never last on a boiled egg.'

Every morning a tin appeared on the table and when I opened it in the staffroom the teachers gathered like bees to honey. It was full to the brim with sandwiches and Club Milks. They got a terrible death from the healthy appetites around me, and Sister was overjoyed at the empty tin. I believed that my first ministry was to the staff and became good friends with many of them. The normal awkwardness between males and females seemed to be cancelled out by the collar, but in its own way the very ease of the relationships marked me out as different.

Clare was from the Southside but apart from that, as

I often told her, she was all right.

'For a mongrel you're very saucy,' she'd retort. 'Wasn't your own father from the Southside?'

Clare brought me home to a house in the lee of the South Chapel, where I could drop anchor with her family and boyfriend and be ordinary. John and Marie brought me to the Opera House and came back to the flat for the night supper. In her innocence Marie asked me to do something on child development with her class. Fired with enthusiasm, I began to draw a womb on the board and a foetus floating in amniotic white chalk. The girls, who were always years ahead of the boys, concentrated on looking superior. The boys' jaws sagged on the desks. By the grace of God, the school inspector walked in the door. He must have wondered at how quiet the children were and why the teacher kept manoeuvring to block his view of the board. Sensibly, Marie never asked me to talk to them again.

The children were second-generation Northsiders with all the subversive wit of their elders. One day I noticed a lad had brought his dog to school. The dog was a few steps above Dinky on the evolutionary ladder but a little to the left of any recognisable breed.

'What d'ya tink of me dog, Father?'

'He's, eh, very interesting, Mick. What did you call him?'

'He have no name.'

I launched into a lecture on how a dog had to have a name. How could he have any identity or dignity without a name?

'Watch him now, Father. Here, stupid.'

The little dog zoomed to his master, propelled by his stump of a tail. Who needed a formal name when you could be hailed in the community with 'sham' or 'bater' without ever losing your dignity?

I revelled in the energy of the place, helping Maurice with the musical and whirling the youngest ones on to the floor at the discos. After the all-boys schools, it was a culture shock to encounter a mixed group. I discovered that while the lads were going through early adolescence properly preoccupied with football, the girls were years ahead in terms of emotional development – twelve going on twenty-seven. Around that time we had an influx of 'refugees' from the North. Sharon was a 'wee' lass with enormous composure. She set her sights on the lankiest of the lads and decided that they were 'going steady'.

'Aren't you a bit young to be doing a steady line, Sharon?'

'Och, Father, sure I'm nearly thirteen so I am.'

Seamus was blissfully unaware of his romantic status. Like most of his group, he had all the coordination of a newborn foal. In his scheme of things, football was God and girls were a distraction. Sharon would not be side-tracked. I found Seamus pressed into a corner one day while Sharon blocked his escape with implacable determination. He gave me a beseeching look.

'Father, for the love of God, will you take her away outta that?'

Apart from cooling Sharon's ardour and saying class Masses, I wondered what my real function was as their priest. Then I remembered something from my childhood that dispelled my worries. When we were very young my eldest sister Kay was going to dances with her friends from school. Sheila, Eily and Anne always came back to our kitchen for the post mortem. As soon as we heard their voices in the kitchen, we three younger ones would tiptoe in our pyjamas to the top of the stairs and huddle behind the banister, sitting on the cold lino risking piles, trying to muffle our laughter at the vivid expressions from below.

Sometimes Kay would check the stairs. 'Are ye up there?' Michael and I had to gag Bernie before she could answer, 'No, we're not.'

I remember one particular night someone mentioned that an older girl was getting engaged. As soon as the fella's name was mentioned, the others went into spasms of disbelief. 'What does she see in him?' they wondered. Years later I asked Kay if that couple had actually married.

'They did.'

'And how did he turn out?'

'Well, he turned out a marvellous husband. He hands up all his money and he's very good with the children.'

As I reflected on the story, I began to realise that the girl had seen whatever was best in that lad. Every time she spoke to him 'twas to the best in him and, of course, the best in him grew to fullness. I developed a motto from the story: 'Whatever you shine your light on will grow.' If I wanted to see cafflers, blackguards and problem children, there would be no shortage of candidates, but I would never see beyond the actions to the real child and never be an agent for growth for any child.

Like any child, I brought stories home from school. To the patients they were pictures from a lost world and I warmed myself to their delight. Often a hand would reach from under the covers to mine and a voice would ask, 'How's the young one you asked us to pray for, Father? Did she pass her exam?'

'She did, Mick.'

'Ah, thank God,' he'd say with a contented smile.

It worked the other way as well. The children often asked me about the hospital and the patients and would punctuate my stories with, 'Ah God help us!' or 'Sure, Gawdy love us.' But a young one, on the verge of tears, once entreated me, 'Ah, Father, don't be tellin' us them stories any more about the old people. Sure you'll draw a fit of depression down on top of us.'

I began to realise that many of them lived in the new housing estates that spread like spokes from the hub of the school. Most of their grandparents lived in the more settled areas, so it was unlikely that the children would see sickness at first hand. I wondered how they'd respond to a real live sick person and made Jim Keating an offer he couldn't refuse.

'Jim, I'm saying Mass on Thursday for the children in Mayfield. Would you come up and give me a hand?'

The same day, a group of his butties were holding court in the bedroom. Led by Colm, the taxi-driver, they were measuring him for the coffin. Very carefully they ran a twine down his length in the bed and matched it to the door.

'Keating, we'll never get you out that way. We'll have to move the jamb.'

Jim played his part to perfection.

'But lads, ye can't leave me here. I have a deposit paid on the plot in Curraghkippawn. Anyway, the neighbours will complain.'

There was much mock scratching of heads all round and then, inspiration.

'Keating,' says Colm, 'when you feel death comin' on ya, could you lean over a bit sideways like in the bed, so that when you stiffen up we can angle you out the door?'

We all laughed heartily at that. It was only through such outlandish rituals that we could cope with the thought of losing him.

The following Thursday he was gleaming in a white shirt, sitting ready in the wheelchair.

'What'll I say to them?'

'Don't worry, Jim,' I said. 'You'll know when the time comes.'

There was nearly a small riot when they saw the wheelchair, and eventually we had to have a draw for the driver. The classroom was festive with posters, the makeshift altar awash with flowers. Uncharitably I wondered which local garden was the unsuspecting donor. But as the woman from Blarney Street said to the post office mistress when she queried her sending a turkey by surface post to the son in Australia, 'Sure, 'tis the thought that counts.'

After the gospel I introduced him.

'Boys and girls, this is Mr Jim Keating. I grew up around the corner from him and, since I was a child, he has always been my great friend.'

Then I sat down. Jim started to speak in his gentle, earnest voice and they leant forward to listen. Without a shred of self-pity he told them about his sickness and how he tried every day to cope with it. He spoke of good neighbours who brought the *Examiner* in the morning and the *Echo* in the evening, and faithful friends who called in casually on the way home from work. It was a lesson in love that I didn't have the personal authority to teach, and, like the children, I sat humbly at the feet of a practising Christian. When he finished there was wild clapping and not a few tears. They crowded around to shake his hand and I winced at their hearty handshakes, knowing how much pain even the slightest pressure could produce. He showed no sign of it, smiling and nodding his head in benediction.

When I got him back to bed he was grey with exhaustion. I think he read the guilt in me.

'Sit down there, boy, for a minute.' He patted the bed beside him.

'I have plenty of time for rest, all right? That was a great privilege for me today and I won't forget you for it.'

He leaned forward and kissed me on the cheek.

'D'ye know what?' he said suddenly. 'I think I'll stand for pope.'

9

THE CHILD IS FATHER TO THE MAN

A span of three long winters, I have known,
November on November, and alone
Have walked among the phantoms etched in gloom,
My sky, the void above the light,
My world, the shadowed room.

And I have heard the secrets of the ones
Who throng about the threshold of the grave,
Who hang old hurts about the sapling-man
And sway his heart to shrive and salve and save.

And when, at last, their winter thawed to spring
Their mortal husk, soft-folded into clay
I stayed behind, a bird of bonded wing
My flock all light-wing wheeling
And away.

After a seven o'clock Mass for the nuns on Sunday
morning, I said another on the hill for the people who
lived in the high houses that stepped in ragged formation

from the barracks to the railway station. Theresa, a lean whippet of a woman, sold the papers from inside a wooden hut at the church gate.

'Lovely day, Father. Dere's to be a coalition government and 'tis full of doctors. You'll have to have a prescription to get a house.'

I got the *Press* and *Independent* every Sunday. Old habits die hard and I came from a crowd who bought both, despite their regular complaint: 'There's nothing in either of them.' Theresa just looked at me when I offered to pay, and I was casting about for some way to counter this when she said, 'Himself wants to be an altar boy.' I was at a loss to know how Theresa's husband could be exalted to that position, when she nodded meaningfully at the counter. The top of a small head loomed like a rising moon from behind a stack of papers and two pale eyes held me steady in their sights.

'Would you like to be an altar boy?'

The eyes blinked.

'Send him in next Sunday before Mass, Theresa, and I'll sort him out.'

'Twas a done deal.

Himself arrived earlier than the others and I had time to get a good look at the rest of him. The round head was perfectly matched by a perfectly round body with legs and arms that looked as if they were stuck on as an afterthought.

'You're welcome,' I said. 'Put on the gear now, like a good boy.'

He blinked. He was a man of few words and had

obviously used all of them. I tried every tack I knew to cajole a few words from him, to no avail. If there was ever a lull in the conversation, he planned to be in the thick of it.

Himself rolled out on to the altar like a roly-poly pope and presided from the bench while the others trotted about their business. For every yin there's a yang, and himself had an exact opposite in Michael. Michael's mouth ran like a tap in the sacristy and he just lowered the volume on the altar. One Sunday, while I was getting my sermon notes in order, Michael paused for breath and himself spoke. It had the same effect on us as the burning bush had on Moses. Even Michael suffered a complete stoppage with shock.

'Father,' himself said in a growly voice, pointing at Michael, 'I hates dat boy.' His eyes had the sort of tight expression I remembered seeing on the hurling pitch when plastic surgery was imminent.

'Ah no,' I said hastily. 'You might dislike him but you don't hate him.'

Himself was implacable. 'I hates him,' he said evenly. 'Dat boy is a disturber.' He was off like a Jack Russell terrier after a rabbit. The 'disturber' read the danger signals faster than me and was already climbing up on to the vesting bench for sanctuary.

'Get him off me,' he screamed.

I had himself in a headlock, trying to keep my hand away from his teeth, and Michael was screaming from the bench, 'He bit me, Father. He bit me. I'll get the lockjaw', when the parish priest sailed in the door. Everyone turned to stone before the gorgon. *Macbeth* had always been my favourite Shakespearean play and this man had been my teacher.

> 'We are in blood
> Stepp'd in so far, that, should we wade no more,
> Returning were as tedious as go o'er'

he paraphrased, and turned tail on the confusion. The Mass bell rang.

A very flushed and dishevelled procession emerged before the unsuspecting congregation. Every few minutes I stabbed the two gladiators with dagger looks to keep manners on them. When I lifted the veil of the chalice, I found that I had forgotten the paten in all the confusion.

'Psst.' Himself appeared at my elbow.

'Whass wrong?'

'I forgot the paten. Will you go in for it, please?'

'Whassa paten?'

'The round goldy thing for the top of the chalice.'

'Why didn'cha say so?'

He had not forgiven my intervention. A genuine Jack Russell must never be disturbed at the kill.

After Mass I coursed him out to Theresa, intent on revoking his hunting licence.

'Isn't he dotey on the altar, Father? D'ye know what, I think he'd make a priest.'

One bad word from me and himself would be history. In the best Northside tradition, Theresa would drive straight over him and reverse in case she missed a bit. Then she would dance on his corpse for 'making a show of her'.

'Actually, Theresa,' I said, 'I was thinking myself what a great bishop he'd make. He has all the right qualities.'

She glowed. Himself blinked one eye. We were friends.

Around this time I got friendly with Ronnie and the two Mauras. The three gangly teenage girls were regular visitors to the patients and I was touched by the way they leant in close to catch a fading voice. They seemed to gravitate naturally towards those who had only occasional visitors, and their mad laughter chased the silence for an hour and drew luminous smiles from the shadows. They started to drop into the flat for night supper before heading home.

'Have you any records, Father?'

'Yes. I have Gigli, Mario Lanza – and this one has a brilliant duet from *The Pearl Fishers* with Jussi Björling and Robert Merrill.'

They looked at each other as if I 'had a want in me'.

'Have you any modern ones, like?'

'Well, I have Barbra Streisand.'

'Ancient.'

We compromised on the Beatles. I got to write a sermon while the three ate all my night supper to *Sgt Pepper's Lonely Hearts Club Band*.

Ronnie was the natural leader of the trio.

'Would you come up and talk to the girls in our class?'

'About what?'

'Ah, ye know,' she said awkwardly, 'fellas and stuff.'

'Why don't ye bring them up to the flat on Friday night?'

They were elated. If wisdom is knowing how much you

don't know, then for once I made a wise decision. A priest's family are always the first victims of his pastoral zeal. Kay, my eldest sister, was unflappable. She heard me out over a steaming plate of skirts and kidneys.

'Would you stop inhaling that and ate it before it goes cold. Friday night? Grand. Myself and Caleb will come up.'

On Friday night the flat was strewn with 'young wans' stretched in a comfortable semicircle on the carpet before the fire. After the introductions the silence was deafening.

'Christy, weren't you going to show Caleb the garden?'

'What? Oh right.'

Bemused, I went out with Caleb and the two of us ambled around the lawn.

'What's all that about, Caleb?'

'Sure they'd never talk while we were there,' he said easily.

An hour later we were dizzy from circling the garden. As soon as we came in the door, the talk stopped. After the night supper, the trio stayed behind to tidy the flat.

'How did it go?'

'Grand.'

The conversation was over. What words of wisdom did she give them, I wondered. Did she tell them how she knew for certain that she would marry Caleb? He came up to our house one night to collect her for a dance and she was up to her elbows in the sink, peeling spuds. With two younger brothers, a younger sister and a widower father, she always had a lot to do.

'Caleb, I can't go anywhere until the spuds are peeled for tomorrow's dinner. If you want to wait, the *Echo* is there on the table.'

He took off his coat and rolled up the sleeves of his best shirt.

'You go on up and get ready, Kay. I'll finish the potatoes.'

She knew at that moment that she had found her partner for life.

The flat became a sort of halfway house for the trio and the other youngsters who visited the wards. A 'goozah', in Cork, is an unwelcome third party on a date. My cousin Peter and his girlfriend Kay regularly brought ten goozahs on their dates. They were involved in a Northside youth club and, every week, shepherded a gang of youngsters to visit the wards. Naturally, they came *en bloc* to the flat for the tea afterwards. I remember that one of them turned into a most unlikely angel to teach me a lasting lesson.

Cancer usually hides inside a person and rarely gets in the way of conversation. Jerry's lump loomed on the top of his head. I tried to ignore it but it was huge, and every time I looked at him my eyes were drawn to it. I made a special effort to look elsewhere, looking behind and away from him so that the poor man must have thought the room was haunted. And then Timmy joined the youth club. Timmy was a collection of ankles, elbows, acne and neuroses. He was at that awful age when even a mother's love can be strained. On his very first visit to the wards, like a pigeon homing to a loft, Timmy headed for Jerry.

'What happened your head?'

'I have a bit of a lump, boy.'

And that was the first time in months that Jerry was

spoken to as a normal human being.

My Nan often said that some people were 'all eyes and no sight'. In this case it was a perfect description of her grandson, but Timmy's experience converted me. Wouldn't it be wonderful if even very young children could have easy access to the patients? Wasn't it bad enough for a terminally ill man to be losing his life without losing touch with his family as well? And why should we presume that because they were old or dying, they had lost their *grá* for children?

I had it all worked out.

Mamma was a brick wall.

'No. You couldn't have children seeing cancer.'

'But, Mother, children are the only ones who don't see cancer.'

'No.'

We needed a miracle to melt her opposition.

It was May, and the children of the parish made their First Holy Communion.

I was drafted in to help with the First Confessions. The girls sang their sins with something approaching pride, and the boys trembled on the brink of involuntary liquidation. The sun smiling on their big day lured them to blossom on our lawn for photographs. Moving among the parents, I happened to glance up at the front of the building. I was transfixed. Every window framed a face. There were men and women up there who rarely bothered to leave the bed, and yet on this special day the beauty and joy of young voices called them from their shadows.

I found her in a circle of tiny brides.

'Mother, will you look up there.'

She looked for the longest moment.

'I suppose you'll give me no peace anyway,' she smiled, and our doors swung open to the angels.

And there were doors of comfort open to me also.

The families on the hill encouraged me to call. After a hectic day, I could kick my cares away playing soccer with the O'Connells in the lane. I could be pleasantly humiliated at Scrabble by Nuala or tied in theological knots by her daughter. Elaine was a member of a running club and full of missionary zeal to spread their painful gospel.

'Will you come for a run?'

We drove out to the Powder Mills in Ballincollig and started with exercises. When I was completely exhausted she said, 'Right, that's the warm-up done, now we'll run.'

Pride is a terrible thing. I rushed to keep up with her long, graceful stride. By the time we started on the second lap, I was beyond agony. I had hit 'the wall' so many times it was beginning to hit me back.

'How did the Church move so far from the simplicity of the apostles?' she asked.

I dropped to my knees, gasping like a mullet strawk-hauled on the North Gate Bridge.

'Are you hyperventilating?'

'No, I'm dying. Listen, Elaine . . . ' I managed, when my breathing had settled down to the merely asthmatic. 'I can run or I can talk theology, but not together. And another thing, could we run together? If I'm behind you, they'll think I'm running after you, and if I'm in front of you, you'll get a bad name.'

She kept that pact for another lap before she laughed, 'If St Paul had done a bit of running, the readings on

Sunday would be a lot shorter,' and she was off again like a greyhound.

On Sundays, when the three Masses and Benediction were over, I could go to my cousin Nora's. She lived in a small, warm house, angled on a hill within sight and smell of Murphy's brewery.

'Go up to Willie's bed. I'll call you for the tea.'

It was enough to watch the telly, anonymous among my own, until the phone rang again to call me back. Nora sprinkled me with holy water at the door, patting my overcoat against the cold. I always glanced in the mirror at the brewery corner, to catch a final glimpse of the small woman, limned in light, her hand upraised in blessing, a talisman against the dark.

It began to dawn on me that I was adopted. Ronnie, the Mauras and the youth club came and went at will, but the Campbells had squatters' rights. Frank and Dave, my two foxy altar boys, had foxy sisters and brothers who wandered easily in and out of the flat. The three youngsters, Dave, Frank and Dorothy, ate all my biscuits, and the older ones balanced their depredations with home-made apple tarts. They were happy to watch the telly, sailing on the mat before the fire, while I read in the armchair, and they would let themselves out across the hill when I was called to the wards.

Seven years in the company of one's peers is no preparation for the reality of children. The *Echo* announced that *Hamlet* would be on the telly, with Laurence Olivier agonising around Elsinore. I got the jobs finished early, the telly and teapot warmed, the armchair angled for a night with the bard. Shakespeare was 'big' in the Northside thanks to Father O'Flynn and the Loft Drama Group. Not everyone was enamoured of Father O'Flynn's obsession. Two elderly ladies were stationed one day in Mulcahy's fresh meat shop in Shandon Street, conferring on the 'seed, breed and generation' of everyone who passed the window. Just then Father O'Flynn hove into view, in what P. G. Wodehouse would have described as a 'dignified procession of one'.

'Moll,' said one, 'would you look at Father O'Flynn, and he tryin' to walk like Shakespeare.'

The productions in the Opera House were usually lavish and well-acted, before an audience of Leaving Cert boys and girls who were much more interested in the dramatic hormonal tension among themselves. The director always managed to iron the spiky accents of Cork into a passably level tone, until the night the messenger missed his cue during a production of *Macbeth*. There was a long dramatic pause and then the hapless fellow rushed onstage to announce, 'De Queen, me Lord, is dead', in an accent that had all the grace notes of Blarney Street.

The production on the telly was the genuine article and I was ready for a feast of culture when the doorbell rang. Three foxy heads bobbed expectantly in the porch.

'Come in quick. The tea is in the pot and the Club Milks are in the tin. Hush now, let ye.'

They grouped on the mat before the fire.

'Who's he, Father?'

'That's Hamlet, Prince of Denmark.'

'Who's yer wan?'

'That's his mother, Gertrude. She married his uncle when he killed his father.'

'Jay,' they chorused, exhaling crumbs on the carpet.

'And who's yer woman?'

'Oh, for the love of God, that's Ophelia. She's doing a line with Hamlet but she'll go mad and drown herself.'

'I wouldn't blame her,' Frank said with feeling, watching Olivier talking to a skull. The philistines were out in force tonight. I turned it off.

'Will we play cards?'

Sometimes their Mam and Dad would come to hunt them home and stay for tea.

'Are they driving you mad, Father?'

'No, but ye can drop over the children's allowance book.'

Almost imperceptibly, they widened the warmth of their family circle to include the priest. Like a grand-parent, I could always ruin them and hand them back, but without their laughter the flat contracted and grew cold. I quizzed my motives for keeping an open door for all who came to call, and admitted before God that I was selfish. I had grown to love their company and was frightened to find that I felt less and alone without them. The books were some solace but the groaning shelves bore testimony to time spent alone. With the turn of a switch I could have Gigli or Streisand for company, but when the needle lifted from the last track the silence seemed deeper than before. Many's the night I sat the fire out, watching the last spark until it grew too tired to glow. This was the lot of the priest, I thought, to be available to all and belong to none.

'You must pray.'

The voices of spiritual directors echoed from the

seminary. I opened up this pain as prayer, spreading it out in the dark before God. But God seemed to have followed the laughter to sit 'where two or three were gathered', and warm himself to their companionship. And who could blame Him?

10

ALL FALL DOWN

And there were silent evenings,
Sitting sightless with a book
The heart-eye, parsing through
A Braille of scarcely dented beds.
When pressure of their hands
Would set my hand-heel
Grinding in my eye
And all the reasons why
Just swept around the steady stone
Of their blind pain
And mine.

The Kerryman declared that he was God.

'How do you know?' the neighbours enquired cautiously. 'Well,' said he, 'whenever I say my prayers, I feel I'm talking to myself.'

Sometimes the boundaries between who you are and what you do become blurred. A priest can be seduced into thinking of himself as pivotal to the work and begin to fill the spaces with it to keep them clear of doubt. He can run so fast that he outpaces thought and falls finally into bed, convinced by his exhaustion that he has 'run the race and won the prize'. That man was me.

The work became my painkiller and my pride. Rushing to and fro gave me the illusion of achievement. Time was hot money; it would burn holes in my hands if I held it fast, and when 'twas spent there was always more that could be borrowed from the night before and the morning after. But there is no sweet music from a string too tightly wound. Time with one patient became time taken from another, and unconsciously I developed a measurement of needs and pains. There was a hostel connected to the hospital by a short corridor. It was a place where elderly ladies could recuperate after an illness or retire to if they wished.

John died slow and hard late in the night and his death-rattle was still echoing in my head when the call came from the hostel in the morning.

'One of the ladies would like to see you.'

The short connecting corridor was a decompression chamber between one world and another. The building was beautifully appointed, many of the residents kept their own furniture, and the room I entered was heavy with mahogany. The lady was gentle and welcoming.

'D'you know, Father,' she said, 'I can't get any good out of that geranium.'

Mentally, I held up the yardstick of John and his killing cancer against this woman and her wilting plant. It was no contest. I thought, wouldn't I love to have your worries. I had forgotten my Nan's wisdom that 'everyone's pain is their own'. But personal pain consumes the available energy as fire devours air; it can cause the heart to contract in contemplation of itself. This was the dark I had feared since childhood and I carried it now inside me in the broad light of day.

It's a fortunate priest who is never 'the priest' to his own. When I rushed into Kay's for a fast cuppa en route to somewhere else, she looked up from the sink.

'God help us,' she said tartly, 'but here's a watch wearing a man.'

My younger sister only saw her brother when he needed a haircut. When Michael woke me with calls from New York, his usual good humour foundered in the shallows of my silences. I took my darkness to my father and fidgeted on the oilcloth until he said, 'Wouldn't you take it a bit easy, boy? You have the weight of the world on you.' Defensively, I listed the litany of needs and night-calls, until he raised his hand in defeat. 'You'll be damn-all good to them dead.'

The spirit works in mysterious ways. I didn't die heroically, like Damien of Molokai. I just slipped the cartilage in my knee.

It happened first in Maynooth. Fifteen of us were attempting plastic surgery on fifteen of them. In the seminary this passed for hurling. I slipped and fell and couldn't rise, noticing with a sort of detached curiosity that my knee was cocked at an interesting angle. The surgeon in the Mater banged it enthusiastically with his fist and announced to his nodding entourage that I was 'an interesting meniscectomy'. The radio played the 'Hallelujah Chorus' as I was trolleyed to theatre, and before I went to sleep the man in green asked me to indicate the knee for the op.

Our college doctor was known to the students as Game Ball. This was his optimistic response to almost all ailments presented, except mine. 'You'll never hurl again,' he said cheerfully. 'Take up golf.' The young physio in the Mater would have been ejected from the SS for being too rough, but she had me back walking in no time. 'Motivation is everything,' she'd say as I sweated under the weights. I had the greatest motivation in the world. I couldn't wait to get away from her before she killed me altogether. In four weeks I had swapped the crutches for the hurley and was scourging a sodden *sliotar* on my own, willing the leg back to par. But Game Ball proved a prophet of sorts. The game that should have saved me was my downfall.

While I was in St Patrick's, Michael's second son was due into the world and I rushed across the Atlantic to christen him. Ivan wisely stayed in the womb until I was well over the Atlantic on my way back, but I did play one round of golf before leaving. We teed off in Mosholu Park and when I swung there was an old familiar pop and my leg was on a separate contract again. On my return to Ireland the nuns hurried me to the Orthopaedic Hospital in Cork. For the first few days after the op I fretted from inactivity. The nurse in charge of the ward was a formidable lady. She had a look that could wilt a young nurse at fifty yards and a voice that could clear visitors like smoke in a draught. 'There was a great barmaid lost in you,' I told her when I got to know her better.

'D'you know who make the worst patients?' she asked.

'Would it be doctors?'

'No. And they're bad enough, God knows. No, the worst in the world are missionaries.'

'Why so?'

'Well, they spend all their time fretting to be back on the missions baptising black babies, and because they can't they make life miserable for the craythurs here who must look after them.'

Point taken.

'I heard you were plastered?'

Pat was as chirpy as ever.

'How are things in the hospital, Pat?'

'Marvellous altogether. Mamma got the loan of a Dominican and he's anointing everyone. I'd say he's in dread of her.'

So the place hadn't ground to a halt after all.

Early the following morning a hush spread in the corridor outside and it was no surprise when the bishop walked in. I was reading a novel called *The Kapillan of Malta* and felt a vague sense of relief that there was a picture of a priest on the cover. As we swapped small talk I began to rehearse my script. This was a God-given chance to tell him that the day couldn't be stretched to take in my list of duties. As I drew breath he asked, 'Does anyone visit Glasheen School?'

'I don't know,' I stammered.

'Would you add that to your list.' He paused at the door and smiled. 'I'll pray for you,' he said calmly and was gone.

As soon as his footsteps faded I couldn't hold it in any longer. Two young nurses rushed into the room. 'What's wrong with you, Father?' But I was laughing hysterically and couldn't answer them. Gradually the madness died down and I wiped my eyes on the blankets.

'Can we do anything for you, Father?'

'Ye can. Would ye ever wash my hair? I haven't been able to shower since I came in and I feel like Murphy's pup.'

I started laughing again and they backed out of the room. I was remembering one of my Uncle Christy's stories about Dinnie and the jennet. Dinny was a character from 'long 'go' who kept a jennet in the house. He was also noted for his meanness.

'D'ye know,' Uncle Christy would say drolly, 'just when Dinny had the jennet trained to live on nothin', didn't he die!' I wished I had told the bishop that story.

They came back with a basin and shampoo and set about the head. It was the first time in a long time that I felt relaxed and the first time that I had let anyone minister to me.

The remaining days were blissful. Nurse brought a small table, and a collection of crocks on crutches staggered in for Mass. I discovered the children's ward one day by accident as I backed through double doors on the crutches. Two rows of miniature convicts peeped at me from behind the bars of high-sided cots. A balloon dithered forlornly on the floor in the middle of the passageway.

'Man,' a tiny boy called from his cell. 'Man, will you get my balloon?'

For what other purpose would a man spend seven years in a seminary? It was my finest hour. Balancing on the good leg, I extended the crutches and gripped the balloon between the rubber tips. Then, with the bad leg stuck out backwards for ballast, I raised the balloon and dropped it in the cot. Nureyev couldn't have done it better and I was half disappointed at the lack of applause, but they were goggle-eyed with admiration. Then a shower of balloons sailed out of every cot in the ward. I beat a hasty retreat.

My room began to resemble the front window of Nosey Keefe's shop with all the fruit brought by the visitors. I decided to share my bounty and made regular pilgrimages to the cots with oranges and grapes. This corporal work of mercy was brought to an abrupt end when a flushed nurse laid down the law. 'Would you stay out of the children's ward. We're changing nappies by the new time.'

All too soon it was time to go back.

11

ENTRANCES AND EXITS

We were walking on a high-ditched boreen west of the city. I was striding as I remember my father doing when we were children, leaning into the road as if to outpace his pain and wear it down. We children would stop to admire a feather-galleon on a pool and race to catch him up, irritated at his unrelenting pace. Now I was the pacemaker. Con, a retired scoutmaster, erect and precise, prodded the road suspiciously with his stick. The Doc flapped along beside him, a black-sailed schooner in a fitful wind, tacking wildly to the sudden gusts of argument. They were going through the comfortable ritual of reminiscing about scout camps in the past that were one step away from typhus in terms of hygiene but were peopled with incredible characters.

'D'you remember the donkey, Con?'

'Will I ever forget?'

I could have whistled this one. The scouts were camped in Tom Deane's field beside a stream that fell from the high fortress of Cahirconree and emptied into Tralee Bay. After an uneventful week the local garda meandered in on his bicycle and, after exchanging the formalities of weather and football, announced that there was a dead donkey upstream. 'He must be there a week,' he said easily, and politely refused the cup of tea before side-pedalling off again, his duty done. This was the stream the camp drew water from to wash, drink and cook.

'You never saw such gawking in all your life.'

The Doc stopped in the middle of the boreen to catch his breath before taking up the narrative. One of the scout leaders shanghaied a troop and borrowed a rope to deal with the dead donkey. The same man was known to have a delicate stomach but as they neared the spot he gathered his courage and rallied the troops.

'Now, lads, just remember ye're scouts and must act like scouts.'

'Oh sir, looka de donkey in the water. He's manky.'

'Gawk,' went the leader.

Eventually the young fellas waded out to the carcass and lashed the rope to a hind leg. Just as the leader was surfacing for air, the lads heaved and the back leg of the donkey parted company with the rest of him.

'Gawk.'

Con and the Doc were now convulsed in the middle of the road, while I marked time with impatience.

'Are we walking or what?'

Doc levelled his stick at me. 'Con,' he thundered, 'that young pup thinks he's the Curé of Ars.'

'And he died roaring,' Con replied blithely.

'He did not, ye bleddy pagan,' the Doc spluttered, 'but that ordained eejit will die young on us.'

There was no let-up. Back in Con's kitchen the Doc

worried at me like a terrier. 'Listen, boy, our Divine Lord and Saviour had sense enough to take a rest. Wouldn't you get involved in something?' He picked up the *Cork Examiner*, the Corkman's Bible, and flung it across the table. 'Read that,' he commanded, stabbing an ad on the inside page. The Everyman Theatre Group were looking for people to audition. 'Didn't you do some of that blackguardin' in Maynooth?'

'What d'ya think, Con?' I asked doubtfully.

'Eat the rasher,' he replied diplomatically. 'You're like a pull-through for a rifle.'

John O'Shea loomed large in the shadows of the theatre.

'And your name?'

'Christy Kenneally.'

His eyes dipped down to the collar and back to my face.

'Right eh, Christy. Maybe you'd read the underlined passage for me. Good. Can you do a Dublin accent? Fine. I'd like you to take a part in the play. We're doing *The Plough and the Stars*.'

We were all amateurs except Laurie. She was brought all the way from Dublin to play one of the female leads and we were a bit in awe of her. Over the weeks she melted our reserve with a repertoire of theatre stories. Somehow she was the only one who didn't know what I did for a living. We were waiting our cue one night at rehearsals when she asked me.

'I'm a priest.'

'Ah, go to God!'

'I am.'

'And I thought you had a thing for wearing black.'

'If you two are finished with that particular scene, you might like to join our play.'

'Sorry, John.'

Laurie stayed in a flat during rehearsals and commuted home to Dublin at weekends. She became a regular visitor to my flat and regaled the young ones with lurid tales from the stage. I knew that many of the patients would remember her from *Tolka Row* on the telly and asked if she'd like to visit the women's ward. As we neared the door she paused and closed her eyes. Then she straightened up, took a deep breath and sailed across the threshold like a queen.

She was recognised instantly from the soap opera and soon she was surrounded and bombarded with questions.

'Did he really marry her? Declare to God and she was no oil paintin'.'

'And what about yourself, girl?'

'Ah, you were much too good for that waster anyway.'

I watched her flash among them like an exotic bird from a strange land, and marvelled at the ease with which her aura kept reality at bay for just a precious while.

The cast grew accustomed to seeing me change out of a soutane and into a Volunteer's uniform, and the performances played without a hitch to packed houses until the chaise longue collapsed. The scene demanded that I fight with Nora, my wife, and then lead her tenderly to the chaise longue to make up. I lay back and took her hand, ready to draw her to my manly breast and sing 'Nora'.

When the leg snapped I was thrown backwards with

my feet in the air. The audience gasped. Miraculously I was still aboard the furniture when the dust settled, but at a much more interesting angle. The 'wife's' eyes were out on stalks.

'I thought you got Fluther to fix that thing?' I said accusingly.

'Well,' she answered in a fit of inspiration, 'he didn't.'

I drew her to me and began to sing, 'When I first said I loved only you, Nora'. By now she had moved from shock to hysteria and as she muffled her mad giggles in my shirt her head banged time on my chest.

'How did you get that lovely quaver into your voice?' someone asked afterwards.

News spread to the Green Room and the cast were congregated in the wings at the end of the scene to congratulate the happy couple. Mick McCarthy, a neighbour's child from the Northside, was among them.

'Doubt'ya, boy,' he smiled. 'Maybe you'd try O'Casey's lines tomorrow night?'

But my nights were numbered.

Even Pat was subdued.

'Himself down below phoned while you were out. He wants you to call down at seven sharp tomorrow night. I dunno were you wise to go into that bloody play at all.'

Then he brightened.

'By the way, was that bit with the sofa part of the play?'

I didn't bother to reply; he had cast his shadow on me. 'Himself down below' was a formidable ecclesiastic. By geographical accident I was within the boundaries of his jurisdiction. Even worse, when I called one of the lads for counsel he exhaled loudly on the phone before remarking in a cagey whisper, 'There's two divils in this diocese, boy, and he's both of them.'

At seven sharp I was ushered into 'the presence' by a silent, self-effacing housekeeper. My grandfather would have described the man within as 'a butty little man', but he wore a coloured bellyband and exuded an aura of easy power. He was seated at the far end of his desk when I entered, and motioned me to the chair on the other side.

'I believe you are active, Father?'

He smiled, but the smile never reached his eyes.

'I am.'

'Well, I'm sure you're aware that up to recently, priests were not even permitted in theatre audiences?'

I did know that, and I also knew that they sat in the wings to obey the rule until it died of shame in 1969. I said nothing.

'We are not men who seek the limelight or *admiratio*,' he continued smoothly.

Someone once asked a fella in Blackpool if it was true that all the Glen hurlers were fiery by nature.

'Ah no, boy,' he replied, 'dey all have long fuses but dey burns awful fast.'

I sat on my hands.

'You will of course desist from this pursuit, Father, and there will be no need for the matter to go further.'

Self-preservation is a very strong instinct but I said it anyway. 'I made a commitment to these people to see this current production through. I must fulfil that commitment.'

We locked eyes for a few moments in silence.

'Very well,' he said finally. 'Good evening, Father.'

I found my own way to the door.

Striding up the hill, I began to laugh out loud. Passers-by nodded deferentially, then looked away in embarrassment at the sight of a young cleric under the influence. But I was intoxicated by an old memory that had bubbled up to life. We were at a scout camp in Kerry, two weeks of damp tents and optional food. The scoutmaster was a jovial fella, a bit older than me. The camp had only a nodding acquaintance with hygiene, but once the latrines were dug well away from the tents and liberally blessed with Jeyes Fluid, God was in His Heaven and all was well with the world. This idyllic existence continued until the day the commissioner hove into view. As soon as the car bumped into the field, the bush telegraph beat out the alarm and we strove to put some order on the chaos. It was a wasted exercise.

He sniffed delicately at pots that were scrubbed with gravel from the river and still carried a cargo of sediment, roughage for the next meal. Ropes were loose, pegs were missing and half the young fellas unconsciously offended him by reversing the two-fingered salute. Word went out that we were to gather in a large ridge-tent for evaluation. We found ourselves ringside seats at what turned out to be our scoutmaster's autopsy. The commissioner chanted tonelessly through a long list of infringements, peppering his tirade with 'never in all my years' and 'a disgrace to the organisation'. The only one who seemed unabashed was the scoutmaster. He stood before the fusillade like a shell-shocked soldier, a vacant half-smile hovering on his face. At last, the damage done, 'the wrath of God' departed.

In the mortified silence, the scoutmaster roused himself from his stupor and remarked, 'Yerra, don't mind him, lads. He have worms.'

It wasn't exactly a philosophy for life, but the memory helped to straighten my back and lift my spirits that evening.

An old Cork cynic was known to say, 'God never closes a door but He catches your fingers in it.' But as the stage-door closed another door opened. Aine McEvoy phoned from RTE. Would I do the *Thought for the Day* on radio? I met her in Dublin and she scanned the scripts. 'They're good,' she said slowly, 'but there's something missing. Do you know any sick person?'

'Sure I know loads of them.'

'Yes, but do you know one in particular who listens to the radio?'

I told her about listening to the pope's blessing with Jim Keating.

'Isn't that for the City and the World?' he asked.

''Tis Jim.'

'Sure 'tis for no one really.'

'He's right about that,' she said, 'and that's what's wrong with your scripts; they're for no one in particular. Now, I'd like to meet this Northside philosopher.'

They hit it off immediately. He made her laugh at his condition and she told him her story. Years before she had fallen under the shadow of TB. The doctors held out no hope to her parents and they decided to send her to Lourdes. They saw her off on a stretcher at the railway station, certain that she would come back in a coffin. When she did return they didn't recognise the smiling girl who walked down the platform to meet them.

She decided we would broadcast Mass from the hospital and we went into overdrive to prepare. Our little choir worked themselves 'into oil' and when the great day dawned hundreds of people joined our congregation on air. It had a remarkable effect on the patients. Some dressed up for the occasion, despite the fact that they could not be seen, and the responses were prompt and hearty. A nurse summed up their feelings when she said, 'Sure it put us on the map.' This was a hospital that cured nobody. These were nurses that would never see a patient go home and these were patients who had heard their death sentence in the phrase, 'There is no more we can do for you.' Today they were reaching out to broadcast a message of ordinary heroism and extraordinary love. If they could never go again to the country, then for one special and memorable hour the country came to them.

But I was haunted by the faces at the windows. On the threshold of sleep I would see them mutely looking through the reflection of the world outside. They came to us to die, but what did they do in the meantime? They sat quietly in the wards or made the short pilgrimage to the day room to sit around the walls while the sun moved the shadows across the carpet until it was time for bed again. The visitors were sparks that brightened up the gloom all too briefly and then were gone. The patients went nowhere.

Nurse sighed tiredly into the chair. She plucked a pin two-handed from her cap, shaking out her hair

'Will you have tea?' I asked.

'No thanks, I'll be away home to my bed in a minute.'

'How are your lads?'

'They're there,' she replied philosophically, 'but Paddy is driving us mad.'

Paddy had arrived in the silent ambulance a month before. A spare, quiet man, he lapsed deeper and deeper into silence as the days wore by.

'We can't get a cheep out of him at all, and when we do 'tis only about his cancer. The girls are beginning to avoid him, and who could blame them? Anyway, maybe you can do something,' she said doubtfully.

Having a chat with Paddy was like ladling soup with a fork.

'Grand day, Paddy.'

Nod.

'Will the Glen do on Sunday, d'ye think?'

Shrug.

'Herself was in last night?'

'Yes.'

Sing ye choirs of angels! Paddy actually said something. Now, keep him talking.

'How's she keeping?'

Shrug.

A radio was playing somewhere down the corridor and as we sat in awkward silence two beautiful female voices coiled around each other to spin a sound that stretched across the spaces. They seemed to draw other voices from the shadows, as if the walls themselves wanted to give witness to the men and women who had once come here to die, and whose heroism would never be known. It lifted Paddy from the chair and turned him to the window where the fading day revealed the image of the man he once had been. His hand moved tentatively to touch the glass in a gesture of longing or farewell. His eyes were silver pools. As the voices soared and pulsed a final time and spiralled down to silence, he turned from the window, his face suffused with a rare glow.

'*Lakmé*,' he said, in a tone that tugged my heart.

The following day I met a friend in Patrick's Street. The same fella was known locally as a 'chancer'. A chancer, in Cork, is neither a fraud nor a liar; he is someone who takes creative liberties with the truth. 'Twas said about this fella that if he fell from a fourth-floor window he'd land in someone else's shoes. He also 'found' things. To be fair, he balanced his larcenous nature with a generous heart, after the style of Robin Hood. When he saw me coming he amputated himself from the corner at Woolworths, bobbing and weaving to avoid imaginary bullets.

'C'mere, how are things above?'

'Not bad at all.'

'Good man. Listen, I have something here you might use.'

He plucked an envelope from inside his coat, his eyes constantly roving over my shoulder, and then he was gone. I flipped the top of the envelope and discovered three tickets for the Cork Opera House.

'Nurse, would you like to go to the Opera House?'

She gave me a level look.

'Oh, and we'd be taking Paddy,' I added hastily.

Paddy, very properly, sat between the two of us in the theatre, silent as ever. In the rush to arrange the outing it never occurred to me to check the programme. As the curtain rose my heart sank. 'Twas far from the ballet I was reared. Northsiders loved opera and, as an old neighbour remarked, 'Drama, girl, sure we're never short of that at home.' But ballet ran a poor second to hurling, pigeons, bowling and dogs. I prayed that Paddy would like the music anyway and wondered was it significant that he kept his cap firmly in place for the entire performance.

Nurse came to the breakfast table after Mass to tell the story. She said that Paddy had walked into the day room that morning and announced, 'I was at de bally last night in d'Opera House.'

'What was it like?' they asked when they had recovered from the shock of Paddy's maiden speech.

''Twas de divil altogether,' he declared happily. 'Dere was young wans with half nothin' on 'em hoppin' around and fellas wearin' less dan a hanky hoppin' after 'em, and catchin' up with 'em.' Paddy had decided that the meantime might be worth taking more notice of after all.

They have a phrase in Cork to describe someone who is good company. They say, 'Sure he'd take you out of yourself.' Eily was one of those. Many of our patients got so much attention paid to their sickness that they were tempted to make it their life's work to the exclusion of everything else. There was no fear of Eily doing that. She was a small, shapeless woman with straight grey hair and City Hall glasses. She was also a most defiantly alive human being and she drove the nun in charge to distraction. In Sister's order of creation, nurses did and patients were done to. A nurse who slowed down to chat was suspect. As for a nurse who might sit on the side of the bed, well, Sister didn't have a vocabulary sulphuric enough to deal with that sacrilege. The joke did the rounds that one particular nurse always took a hypodermic syringe with her when she went to visit the patients. As she sat on the bed she'd confide, 'If yer woman comes, you're getting a jab of this.'

As a patient Eily broke the mould and Sister's heart. She insisted on helping with the wash-up or carrying trays to other patients and was thick-skinned enough to ignore looks or sarcastic remarks. She was also an insatiable magpie, hoarding pieces of material from all quarters to make soft toys. Her bed was her warehouse and workshop. The mattress was so high from stored contraband that I asked her if she got nosebleeds during the night. The very first time I was introduced, she said shyly, 'You don't know me, boy, but I know you and all belonging to you.'

'How so, Eily?'

'Sure I'm from Gerald Griffin Street and wasn't I in school with your mother Maura, the light of Heaven to her.'

She had a captive audience from that moment as she wove coloured threads in and out of my fading memories of Maura. Eily went to see me in the play and greeted the cast afterwards like the Queen Mother. Sometimes I linked her down to the flat for her supper and one day I plucked up the courage to ask her if she would come with me to my mother's grave.

It was spring and the ditches along the road to Whitechurch were flickering with wrens and spattered with primroses. 'Pull in there, boy,' she commanded and we plucked handfuls of the delicate blooms to place with our prayers before the headstone. We were easy with the silence on the way back and I was startled when she said, 'D'ye know, I still have me home. Would you like to see it?'

Eily's home had all the look and smell of desertion and decay. The houses on either side, like two good neighbours, did their best to shoulder it upright but it was dying of emptiness. I watched her carefully as she picked her way around the rubble from room to room. She stopped here and there and touched the walls with a tenderness we reserve for old faces which have become precious in their fragility.

'I dunno will I ever come back here,' she whispered. 'The nuns want me to sell up but this is my home and so long as I have it . . . ' Her voice trailed off wistfully and two enormous tears loomed behind her glasses.

'Will we say a prayer for our dead, Eily?'

'We will, boy,' she answered strongly, giving her nose a vigorous wipe.

'For Maura, your mother, and all my own.'

The house seemed to sag when she stepped back over the threshold. She turned at the door of the car to look back. It was a look of such love that I thought, she will bury the lot of us because she has something to live for. And at that moment I envied her that sad old house.

12

LETTING GO

October coughed a few times in the chimney as, outside, a few last hardy leaves flushed hectic red. The change before death. Cork buried itself in a brown smoke-shawl; the city spires loomed, marooned, glinting coolly in a low-slung light. Beyond the wall, tyres pressed dead leaves to patterned mush as children, shapeless in coats and scarves, leant into the wind, tacking reluctantly to school.

Our world contracted. The pallid garden grass was lichen-low; the fingers of bare trees beseeched the sky. Squalls swept the paths of autumn's store. The wind died in the dark; frost formed and silvered up the steps to weep beneath the threshold of the door. And then November came, the dying of the year.

The climate in the wards remained the same but there are also seasons of the heart, and in this dark, cold time so many hearts let go. The phone beside my bed became a thing of dread, waiting to shrill at 4 am when life is at its lowest ebb, to drag me up and out, to hold the man whose chest rose up and down and up and down and stopped.

'Saints of God, come to his aid.'

Norma saw the curtains close and heard the prayer murmur from within. She fled the ward. She had a man and children, three good reasons to defy her death. Her refuge was a wheelchair parked against the corridor wall, and there she kept her vigil, listening for the tread that had to come, but not today. Sweet loving Saviour Jesus, not today.

We sat there, side by side like conscripts bloodied from the line, pulled back to rest awhile. I was too tired for small talk, contented just to keep her company, watching as the last light of day ebbed from the windows and another night began.

'Do you ever get browned off, Father?'

'Sometimes.'

The silence stretched.

'Arrah, Jesus,' she said suddenly, 'we're not dead yet. Come on and I'll give you a race.'

Chair to chair, hub to hub, Messala and Ben Hur, we tensed for off.

'Ready, steady, go.'

We strained and slapped the rims and flashed along the lino, laughter flaring like a ribbon in our wake, and crashed together in a wreck beyond the nurse's station, wheezing for air. And there beyond the pane, squat and small, was the mortuary.

'I suppose 'tis out there for me, Father?'

Somewhere in the race, we had crossed the bounds of priest and patient.

'Is there something I can do?'

'The kids are very small. Mike is a good man and I

know they'll want for nothing. Maybe they'll forget?'

Her eyes beseeched the only answer I could give.

'No, Norma, they won't forget. My own mother died when I was five. I miss her to this day.'

She nodded and tried to smile. Slowly she sat upright in the chair and smoothed her dressing-gown.

''Tis time to go back inside.'

For three endless weeks I broke the Body of Christ into smaller and smaller pieces as they held her upright to receive. The morning came when nurse just shook her head inside the door. Mike sat, awkward in his big overcoat, his open face creased with waiting. As I bent to touch her cheek she tugged her eyes open.

'Am I dying, boy?'

'Yes, Norma. Mike is here now and he'll stay with you.' She took our hands and turned to face her husband.

'Will you say the prayers, Father?'

The stilted words were ashes in my mouth. I faltered to a halt, laid down the book and prayed. 'This is a good woman, Lord. She has been a good wife and mother, loved by her own, and by those of us who have come to know her. She has suffered enough. We give her into your peace. Grant her rest now and let her go.'

Mike stretched across the bed and squeezed my arm. 'Thanks, Father.'

This was his place now; it was time for me to leave.

'I'll be below if you want me.'

The frost crunched like pebbles on the path. I felt cold to the bone, hollow and empty. Cork lay below me, asleep beneath the fog, a haze of yellow light rising from the silent docks.

Inside the flat I fumbled for the bottle in the press and drank to melt the lump of ice that lodged inside my chest. As the level dropped, the shadow-places filled with faces, faces leached of colour, luminous with the final flare of life. Faces that were white peaks and dark hollows. And the eyes, always the eyes, fearful or amazed, until they turned inside, untethering the soul. I tried to weave these phantoms into prayer; a prayer that often stumbled into some old comfort tune my father used to quell the demons of the dark.

So tooreloo reloora loora lie bye,
In your Daddy's arms you're creeping
And soon you will be sleeping
Toreloora loora loora loora lie.

A moment's panic as I realised that cracked and quavering voice was mine. I bit down hard upon my fist, fearing that the shakes would let me loose and I might howl and batter hard on Heaven's door and never ever stop.

13

IGNATIUS

A 'wilder' in his day, they said.
Could toe to hand the hard-fought ball
Or tacking through a reef of shoulders
Drop-kick home, to spume their wild applause.
All ebbed to dim reflection
In the body that betrayed him,
Took his legs and predeceased him,
Made his sky a patch of ceiling.
This Brother taught Melchisedech to dance
To watch the blossoms bud between the tombs
And when my steps moved surer to the tune
I heard him laughing.

There was an odd camaraderie among those who dealt in death, a rough and covert kindness that helped us take the strain. Like the Masons, we had our secret signs: a nod across the empty bed, a china cup of tea, conjured from among cracked mugs, a soft 'God keep you' at the closing of a late-night door. The undertakers assumed their rightful place among our group. Vested in sombre black, they moved through rituals as reverently as any priest, ambassadors between the living and the dead, ever watchful for the smallest deed that might assuage the pain. The O'Connors were an integral part of Northside life and death, held in wry esteem by generations of potential customers. The older folk engaged in the sort of banter people use as a defence against the inevitable day.

'Hello, Mr O'Connor.'

'Hello, ma'am. How are you?'

'I'm grand, thank God. You needn't measure me at all yet.'

They measured, boxed and buried someone for all of us and were known to lose the bill when times were hard or someone hadn't 'chick nor child'. These mild-mannered men had an avuncular affection for the young priest. I remember one of them taking me for a stroll in the cemetery one wet day after a burial.

'Don't take me up wrong now, Father,' he said gently, 'but have you an overcoat?'

'I have,' I said defensively, 'but the oul' anorak is warmer.'

'Well now, that's true, but everyone else wears an overcoat for funerals. 'Tis more respectful, like.'

The petrol strike grounded my car and I took the bus to school. Riding upstairs, looking into back yards or steering the bus with the metal bar at the front had always been pleasures of my childhood.

'Hello, Christy boy.'

Fonsy, a great Glen hurler in his day, swayed up between the seats, his conductor's purse swinging on his hip like a gunslinger's holster. He plonked his feet on the floor and parked his bottom on the rail.

"Tis seldom enough we get one of ye,' he smiled.

'How much do I owe you, Fonsy?'

'Go away and have sense. Tell your father I was asking for him.'

I sat in dread of an inspector until we reached my stop and the bus exhaled me onto the pavement. I resolved to walk from then on but I couldn't walk to funerals. Mr O'Connor anticipated my problem. 'Go in the hearse with the lads.'

It was a funeral with a difference. Bertie was eighty years old and an orphan. At least he had none of his own that we could trace when he died as quietly and anonymously as he had lived. The graveyard was outside Mallow, a twisting twenty miles away from Cork, and I sat between the driver and his helper in the silver hearse. Conscious of Bertie lying in state behind, we were a bit subdued on the way out, steering the small talk into the safe waters of sport. The graveyard itself was a jungle of briars and tumbled stones. Apart from the officials, the two nuns from St Patrick's were the only mourners. There was a few bob somewhere in Bertie's family tree and he was to be interred in a vault. We had a moment of confusion as the undertaker searched for the entrance.

'Hello,' cried a voice from a nearby headstone, and a character emerged like Lazarus to the light. He was lanky and lean, a greyhound of a man with long legs in outsize wellies and a cap on his head that looked welded.

'De dead arose and appeared to many,' the driver whispered out of the side of his mouth. Undertakers, I discovered, were practised ventriloquists, capable of keeping up a ribald sub-commentary on the most sacred of occasions.

'Are ye lookin' for the door?' the apparition enquired. 'Tis down here,' he shouted and disappeared into a hole. Sure enough there was a small metal door set into the base of the vault wall. Hinges screeched with rust and indignation as our new-found guide forced entry. Eventually the cap emerged from the gloom. 'Dere's no room,' he declared.

'Well, we can't take him home,' one of the undertakers said blandly and jumped down to investigate. After much heaving and shoving, Bertie's ancestors were rearranged in their eternal slumber to make space for their descendant. 'Lave her down to me now,' said our friend, and the coffin was lowered by ropes until he fielded the front end to his chest. The lads upped the rear and pushed. Yer man backed into the vault. When the undertakers had climbed out, they dusted their knees and clasped their hands across their stomachs in readiness for prayer.

'I can't get out,' the voice called tremulously from the tomb. Mr O'Connor had another funeral waiting in Cork. With a flourish, he swept the sheet of plastic grass over the hole in the ground and anchored it with wreaths.

'We'll have the decade of the Rosary now, Father,' he said piously.

Glory be to God, I thought, we're burying a live man. I started the prayers as steadily as I was able. After the first Our Father, I noticed I was on a solo run, as the others coughed into handkerchiefs or leant on each other, laughing silently. At the end of the decade I had four half-moon dents in my palm from digging in my nails to avoid joining them.

The hearse rocked on its springs with high spirits as we sped home to Cork.

'Is this a Rolls, lads?'

''Tis, Father.'

'God, 'tis very quiet.'

'You could do a ton and hear nothing in this, Father.'

There was a straight stretch coming up and, to prove their point, they put the pedal to the floor. The Rolls responded with the exuberance of a pure-bred stallion, normally forced to trot between the traces.

'Lads, aisy on a small bit. What about the guards? We might get a summons.'

'Yerra, we'll say we're on a sick call,' they laughed, and the needle crept higher.

The summons that did come was one I had to answer. Ignatius was a Presentation Brother, bound to the bed by paralysis. He had a quick tongue, a sharp eye and legions of visitors. As well as his brothers of the cloth who tiptoed awkwardly to the wards in regular pilgrimage, he had a line of lay people who came for his counsel. It was as if the paralysis had released him from the inhibitions that curtail the rest of us. Ignatius had served his time in the silence of Melleray before joining the Brothers and when he said something it was because he had something to say. More than one pilgrim got such a straight talking to that it 'cured his cough'. I had no dispensation from his candour; Ignatius took no hostages.

My downfall was determined when I took the high moral ground on gossip. More than once I had a tearful nurse salting the breakfast boiled egg with a sorry tale of 'someone said'. Any institution can fall prey to loose talk and I undertook to use the power of my office to nip it in the bud.

That Sunday morning I closed the gospel and let them sit a moment in silence. I ran my finger slowly along the front of the pulpit, raised my finger to my lips and puffed.

'My dear friends,' I said solemnly, 'it would be easier for me to recover every grain of that dust than it would be for you to recover an unkind word spoken of another.'

The effect was a little spoiled by the fact that no pulpit in a nuns' chapel has ever known a single speck of dust. But they were dumbstruck and I was up and running, warming to my theme. Afterwards, still humming with righteousness, I was summoned by Ignatius.

'Fine sermon, Father,' he said gently. 'But you forgot who you were talking to.' I looked around the ward at souls who were carrying heavy burdens, and realised that my fine words had done nothing to lighten their load. It was an opportunity missed and I felt ashamed.

'Right, Brother,' I said meekly.

'Light a fag for me,' he said firmly and I knew I was forgiven. I lit the cigarette and placed it between his lips, holding the ashtray like an acolyte until the ash drooped like a diviner's rod.

'What do you think of the Jesuits?' he asked suddenly.

'A Jesuit is a man who can eat just one Tayto crisp,' I said lightly, kicking for touch.

'I had one of them here yesterday,' he continued, 'and

he told me that Pope John XXIII would be in purgatory for a million years for calling the council.'

Like most priests of my generation, I had a vague affection for the fat little pope who was elected as a caretaker pontiff and then set about spring-cleaning the Church from spire to crypt.

'I don't agree, Brother.'

He stopped mid-drag on the fag, the smoke crinkling his eyes. I wondered if I had strayed outside the bounds of loyalty to the caste.

'And tell me now, Father,' he said seriously, 'would the likes of me end up in purgatory?'

This was a familiar theme. Many of the older people were so afraid of punishment in the next life that it overshadowed the little bit of life that remained to them here.

'Why would that happen, Brother?'

'Maybe I was a bit of a "wilder" when I was young.'

'Maybe you were. Maybe we all were – and still are. But my father didn't love his saucy caffler any the less for it. And what sort of father would deny his child for being human? Didn't God love our humanity enough to send His son to bless it. No, Brother, there's too much talk about fault and not half enough about love.'

'You're preaching again,' he said, laughing, and added seriously, 'Were you a late vocation?'

'No, Brother, I was early, much too early I think. I got the notion at fifteen and held it. I often wonder would I be a better man and priest if I had waited.'

'"Might have" is a waste of time, boy,' he said firmly. 'I should know. But you're right about love. I see it here all about me in the nurses and the nuns and these other craythurs. I might have run too fast to ever see it if I had legs. You let the fag go out!'

Ignatius became my spiritual sparring partner, jabbing me back to earth whenever I left it. When I preached on daffodils coming up through concrete and talked of hope and the indomitable spirit for growth that God had planted in all of us, he reminded me of the patch of ceiling that was his horizon from dawn to dusk.

'Bring God's love out of the plaster, boy,' he challenged.

I tapped his wisdom as often as I tapped the ash from his cigarette, watching it glow between us like a sanctuary lamp.

I was kicking a ball with children in Mayfield when the call came. The candles were already burning and the oils laid ready. Around his bed the nurses who had turned him like a child knelt on the cold floor, many in tears. As soon as we finished the prayers, he sighed softly and his soul left him. For a moment I had a blurred vision of a young Brother holding his soutane with one hand while he lashed a football against a gable-end. Then I was sitting in the tiny chapel gallery wondering at the blood that poured from my nose to join the tears pooling in my lap.

14

CHRISTMAS

People rarely died at Christmas. An air of expectation seemed to permeate the wards and lighten heavy hearts. Throughout the hospital the transformation started early. Holy pictures sprouted holly as bewildered plaster saints anchored the sagging bunting. Plastic Santa faces bloomed on every door and Pat was obliged to limbo under the massive tree to get in or out of his cubbyhole. Catching him on all fours with tinsel in his teeth, I joked, 'Mecca is the other way.'

But he was already hip-deep in presents and ignored me. Families never forgot the courteous and kindly man who met them at the door of a place they held in dread.

Some people hate the hustle and bustle of Christmas. 'Sure 'tis only the one day' was a familiar refrain. One weary woman toiling up Shandon Street on Christmas Eve, laden down with bounty she could ill afford, was heard to remark, 'Tank God he didn't have a brudder.'

To us it was a time of escape from the round of death and dying. Just as some of our people lived beyond their expected span for a daughter's wedding or to hold a first grandchild, so too would they revive in preparation for the coming of the Christchild. It was a time when we could release the child in all of us, and the hospital buzzed with renewed energy. Every softhearted fella within a three-mile radius who could play the accordion, and more who couldn't, wound up gigging on the wards. Carol singers trooped the corridors to sing outside the doors, their young and rosy faces reflected in tired eyes, cracked and quavering voices joining in their chorus.

This was my third Christmas and my third time calling on Bríd to come and sing for us. She was a most talented singer who performed during the year in Bunratty Castle for the tourist brigade from the States. It was her affliction to be my cousin. This year, like every other, she answered the call and leant on her father, my uncle Joe, to transport herself and the harp to the hospital. As I lugged the harp from ward to ward, I often prayed fervently that she would be converted to the flute.

Bríd brought magic with her. I remember a lady who was on the Brompton Cocktail, a concoction of drugs designed to quell chronic pain. Sometimes it worked and sometimes it didn't. A patient in acute pain has little room in her for anyone or anything else. Her every waking hour is spent shoring up her energy against the next wracking wave of pain and then the next one after that. The nurses were doing their best to bring Lily some small comfort as Bríd set up the harp, and as her fingers stroked the strings to life, the delicate notes soothed the ward to silence.

'Fill, fill, a rún-o,' she sang. The old and plaintive air rose and fell and surged across the lined faces, a wave of beauty washing smooth their cares. It filled the eyes of young and old alike, and stilled. Then Lily whispered, 'Nurse, would you move a little, dear. I want to see that young wan.'

That sea-change travelled with the harp from room to room, leaving a blessed solace in its wake, until we came to Nora.

A month or more before, Nora had given up the fight and lapsed into a listless, almost catatonic state. We had tired of calling her from her private world and contented ourselves with stroking her hand or cheek as we would a calm, daydreaming child. Bríd settled herself on the stool, stilled her mind and leant into the harp.

'Mellow the moonlight to shine is beginning . . . '

And again the small knot of people around the bed were loosened and lost to the soft hypnotic spinning of the wheel. As the last delicate notes trickled off and died, Nora spoke.

'Darling,' she asked in amazement, 'how did you know that this was my favourite song?'

She was back from the dead.

The excitement built to a climax for Christmas Eve and Midnight Mass. In most of the city churches Midnight Mass had moved back to nine o'clock. This was to avoid disruption from craythurs who had drunk 'not wisely but too well'. Sadly, the manger was becoming sanitised of earthy rough and tumble into ritual respectability. Because of our tiny chapel, we were reduced to the painful practice of handing out tickets. But at least we could be sure that those who had been part of our family throughout the year could sit at the table with us on this special night. The families on the hill trooped through the gate to kneel among the wheelchairs or line the walls. The children perched attentively on the altar steps until the little chapel seemed to swell and fill with warmth.

Sitting in the sacristy I could hear the expectant hum as the clock ticked towards midnight, and was wondering what few words I could say that would move through the microphone to the speakers in the wards and carry some measure of solace. Even the altar boys were subdued, as if they sensed the magic of the hour. Then, in a rustle of white vestments, we went out to greet the Child. It was usually a challenge to rescue the ritual from the dullness of overuse, but on this night I found the words startling and sweet and echoed back with strength in the responses. A senior nurse brought all her years of caring to the reading from Isaiah, moving with unpolished authority through promises of better times to come. The simplicity of the gospel story stilled us all to silence. This is not a night for preaching. The Word is best left undiluted by more words. I contented myself with giving the Christ-child into their care, knowing that He would be in good and loving hands. We moved together through the mystery of the Eucharistic Prayer to the Consecration and a trembling of bells. And then they came to claim the Child with outstretched hands and swollen tongues, supported by a daughter, nurse or son.

And afterwards we sat, as friends sit after meals, easy in each other's company, and Bríd sang 'O Holy Night'. For a long time after the last notes had faded, I was afraid to speak and certain that they would be unable to respond. Then I roused myself to bless and let them go. My father and sisters went for tea with the other visitors and I went to the wards.

'We were in Heaven,' Nora said simply, holding the hands of her boy and girl.

Like every other meal, I had the Christmas dinner on my own. It was the way of things then. Throughout the day I watched cars come and go, and children dance to the door, laden with bright boxes. In the evening I saw the last ones leave the pool of light before the door, and watched it close again against another year. The visitors are the true heroes of our story, I thought. The quiet, faithful ones who take the bus and climb the steps in trepidation day after day to sit with Mam or Dad and then retrace their well-worn path across a city innocent of their pain. I see them now as steady stars, glowing in the dark around the beds. I see the twins who came, light-footed out from school to race the stairs and do their 'eck' on either side of Daddy's bed. I see a daughter 'mother' her mother, crooning to her to take a tiny sip as she nestles in the cradle of her arm. I see the three fine sons whose mother had survived the *Lusitania*, keeping loving vigil on the shore as she made ready for her final voyage. In time we'd gather in the mortuary and watch them shoulder Mammy home. Perhaps they'd call once more, a final pilgrimage to collect that small, sad bag of clothes.

The bunting was coiled in the biscuit tin to sleep another year. Winter counted up its toll of empty beds and ceded us to spring. Leaves, young and eager, stretched from tree to tree to shield us from the summer's glare. I had been three years in this place, as unaware of passing time as a boy who hovers with his kite is lost to the spinning of the world beneath his feet.

The priest was a spare, balding man with intense dark eyes barely contained behind his black-rimmed specs. He had a relative in the beds above and concelebrated Mass with me each morning. As we folded our vestments on the bench, he told me he worked in the Catholic Communications Centre in Dublin and was on the lookout for his successor.

'You write a bit, Christy, don't you?'

'I do, Pat, but mostly for my own amazement.'

'You did the *Thought for the Day* on radio?'

'I did.'

'Yes, well, we'll see.'

In the business of the everyday it became a pebble in the shoe, a niggling thought and not much more. The bishop was his usual mixture of warmth and formality.

'I had a request from the Catholic Communications Centre. They want you to work there. Would you go?'

'Do you want me to?'

'I do.'

'Then I'll go.'

There was no other answer. I knew the score. None of us could stake our claim on anyone or any place. This was the cutting edge of priesthood; I could not expect exemption from the blade.

Mamma was quieter than usual. Unexpectedly she accepted the offer of tea and passed no remark on the untouched breakfast before me. We chatted with forced brightness about the new job and how different it would be. I couldn't sustain it and we fell silent again. She placed her cup and saucer on the table and stretched her hand to mine across the cloth. 'We'll miss you, Christy,' she said softly, and left the room.

Pat was like a mother hen, clucking busily in and out of the flat. 'Are you sure you have everything? The key, did you leave the key? Ah sure, I have it here in me pocket. I'm getting bothered.'

He tugged the last box of books into the porch. Now there was no more to be done and we had to face each other.

'My bladder was always too close to my eyes,' he said and held me very tightly. 'You'll come back and see us, boy, some time?'

I couldn't answer him. We could never have our time again and both of us knew that. Another priest would come and grow to love them, and two would be a crowd. My last memory is of looking back over my shoulder at the hospice that had been my home and life for three years and at the statue of the Sacred Heart in the garden. Still pointing at His broken heart and still looking the wrong way.

For three short years
I trod the winepress of their pain
Until I could no longer tell
Whose blood I wore upon my feet.
Their reaching out
Surprised my hidden self to love
To touch, caress and hold
To walk the water
Of a thousand tears
Or sit quite still

In their dark silence
Simply being awake.
The little music I could make
They savoured, stored
And measured back
A hundredfold to me.
And though I banged the Temple door
And flung my 'Why?' before His face
The morning brought me
Humble to the mill
That ground the kernel of their spirits fine
And there was in the wine
The blood their hearts had wept
While mine had slept.
And though I raised them up
With arms of lead
And leaden-tongued
Pronounced the words of life
I glimpsed a gleam of glory there
To spark and flare
Like fire on my clay,
That glazed my dross to shine
For yet another day.